VIVA
Bloom's
NOTES

Ernest Hemingway's
A FAREWELL TO ARMS

Edited and with an Introduction by

HAROLD BLOOM

Viva Books Private Limited
New Delhi • Mumbai • Chennai • Kolkata • Bangalore • Hyderabad

First Indian Edition 2007

VIVA BOOKS PRIVATE LIMITED

- 4737/23 Ansari Road, Daryaganj, New Delhi 110 002
  E-mail: vivadelhi@vivagroupindia.net, Tel. 42242200
- Plot No. 76, Service Industries, Shirvane, Sector 1, Nerul, Navi Mumbai 400 706
  E-mail: vivamumbai@vivagroupindia.net, Tel. 27721273, 27721274
- Jamals Fazal Chambers, 26 Greams Road, Chennai 600 006
  E-mail: vivachennai@vivagroupindia.net, Tel. 28290304, 28294241
- B-103, Jindal Towers, 21/1A/3 Darga Road, Kolkata 700 017
  E-mail: vivakolkata@vivagroupindia.net, Tel. 22836381, 22816713
- 7, Sovereign Park Apartments, 56-58, K. R. Road, Basavanagudi, Bangalore 560 004
  E-mail: vivabangalore@vivagroupindia.net, Tel.26607409, 26607410
- 101-102 Mughal Marc Apartments, 3-4-637 to 641, Narayanguda, Hyderabad 500 029
  E-mail: vivahyderabad@vivagroupindia.net, Tel. 27564481, 27564482

Published by arrangement with

Facts on File, Inc.
132 West 31st Street
New York NY 10001
USA

ISBN 81-309-0449-7

Published by Vinod Vasishtha for Viva Books Private Limited, 4737/23 Ansari Road
New Delhi 110 002. Printed and bound at Anand Sons, Delhi.

Contents

User's Guide

This volume is designed to present biographical, critical, and bibliographical information on Ernest Hemingway and *A Farewell to Arms.* Following Harold Bloom's introduction, there appears a detailed biography of the author, discussing the major events in his life and his important literary works. Then follows a thematic and structural analysis of the work, in which significant themes, patterns, and motifs are traced. An annotated list of characters supplies brief information on the chief characters in the work.

A selection of critical extracts, derived from previously published material by leading critics, then follows. The extracts consist of statements by the author on his work, early reviews of the work, and later evaluations down to the present day. The items are arranged chronologically by date of first publication. A bibliography of Hemingway's writings (including a complete listing of all books he wrote, cowrote, edited, and translated, and selected posthumous publications), a list of additional books and articles on him and on *A Farewell to Arms,* and an index of themes and ideas conclude the volume.

Harold Bloom is Sterling Professor of the Humanities at Yale University and Henry W. and Albert A. Berg Professor of English at the New York University Graduate School. He is the author of twenty books and the editor of more than thirty anthologies of literature and literary criticism.

Professor Bloom's works include *Shelley's Mythmaking* (1959), *The Visionary Company* (1961), *Blake's Apocalypse* (1963), *Yeats* (1970), *A Map of Misreading* (1975), *Kabbalah and Criticism* (1975), and *Agon: Towards a Theory of Revisionism* (1982). *The Anxiety of Influence* (1973) sets forth Professor Bloom's provocative theory of the literary relationships between the great writers and their predecessors. His most recent books are *The American Religion* (1992) and *The Western Canon* (1994).

Professor Bloom earned his Ph.D. from Yale University in 1955 and has served on the Yale faculty since then. He is a 1985 MacArthur Foundation Award recipient and served as the Charles Eliot Norton Professor of Poetry at Harvard University in 1987–88. He is currently the editor of the Chelsea House series Major Literary Characters and Modern Critical Views, and other Chelsea House series in literary criticism.

Introduction

HAROLD BLOOM

The lyric intensity of *A Farewell to Arms* is sustained with enough aesthetic dignity to make the book Hemingway's best novel after *The Sun Also Rises.* Frederic Henry is not an altogether rousing hero; he is depressed, apathetic, devious, disillusioned (of course), guilty, nihilistic, inwardly hostile towards women, and fundamentally quite passive. Catherine Barkley is far more admirable; she is capable of humor, has an uncanny sense of the future, and is stoical and self-sustaining, though a touch improbable. But Hemingway is far more interested in the fairly tiresome Frederic Henry, which would sink the book except that stylistic eloquence and narrative verve combine to make the impressionistic story live, despite the inadequacy of its protagonist, and the apparent idealization of Catherine Barkley. Whether she is over-idealized is ambiguous; her courage is certainly convincing, but most critics are bothered by her simplicity, or these days by her submission to her love for Frederic. There is also a certain feminist resentment that Hemingway kills her off, as it were, but that begins to be fantastic. An elegiac novel requires a victim to be mourned, and so Catherine must die if there is to be a book at all.

Wallace Stevens, the central American poet of this century, thought that Hemingway was essentially a poet. In *A Farewell to Arms,* Hemingway attempted to be a tragic poet; he remarked that the book was his *Romeo and Juliet.* Presumably the Montague-Capulet quarrel is replaced by a Europe at war, but the remark remains rather puzzling: What causes the tragedy, if it can be one, except nature itself, since both Catherine and her infant perish together? Catherine and Frederic are unlucky, and accident does not insure the tragic sense. Hemingway had great difficulty in concluding *A Farewell to Arms;* he wrote version after version, many very different from the one we have now. The text Hemingway chose is purely nihilistic or absurdist; the dead Catherine seems a statue to Frederic, and he walks back to his hotel in the rain. We are left not with tragedy, but with a sense of aesthetic loss.

A sensuous immediacy, a heightened awareness of the colors, odors, and tastes of the world, was the consequence of Catherine's gift to Frederic of her love. Losing her, he loses, whether forever or not we don't know, the enlargement of his world. Apathy will attend his fall into the quotidian, the death-in-life that Hemingway identifies with the conviction of nothingness.

Robert Penn Warren, a distinguished poet-critic-novelist of the generation after Hemingway's, defended *A Farewell to Arms* by arguing that Catherine's death is meant to tell us that "the attempt to find a substitute for universal meaning in the limited meaning of the personal relationship is doomed to failure." It is difficult for me to see what Warren implied: What transcendental, universal meaning do Frederic or Hemingway find in the love affair that ends so darkly, and through no one's sin or error or flaw? Whatever his nostalgias for a transcendental order, Hemingway writes *A Farewell to Arms* out of a conviction that only personal relationships matter. He cannot be punishing *his* Romeo and Juliet for their relationship. Wryly, Hemingway tells us an unhappy story that gives us no comic or ironic relief, which was a much stronger feature in the superior *The Sun Also Rises*. Perhaps *A Farewell to Arms* will not prove to be a permanent book, but for now it retains a kind of lyrical splendor, an unhappy sense of what might have been. ✤

Biography of Ernest Hemingway

Ernest Hemingway was born on July 21, 1899, to Dr. Clarence and Mrs. Grace Hall Hemingway in Oak Park, Illinois. Clarence Hemingway, an avid hunter and fisherman, shared his love of the outdoors with his son each summer at Walloon Lake in northern Michigan, which influenced many of his stories. During the rest of the year, Hemingway attended public school in Oak Park, where he actively participated in athletics and wrote columns in the style of sportswriter Ring Lardner for the school newspaper.

When he graduated from high school in 1917, he skipped college to pursue journalism. For seven months, Hemingway received a valuable on-the-job education as a cub reporter at the Kansas City *Star* but longed to join the American troops overseas fighting World War I. Rejected by the army because of an eye injury, he became an ambulance driver for the Red Cross. In July 1918, he was seriously injured by shrapnel near Fossalta di Piave, Italy, and was decorated by the Italians for his bravery. After recuperating in Milan, he returned to Michigan in January 1919.

Bored with inactivity, Hemingway soon began writing features for the Toronto *Star.* In 1920, he also worked as a contributing editor of a trade journal in Chicago, where he met Hadley Richardson. The couple married a year later and moved to France. Hemingway traveled through Europe as a foreign correspondent for the Toronto *Star* and spent much time in Paris associating with expatriate American writers such as Gertrude Stein and Ezra Pound. After a brief return to Toronto for the birth of his first son, he quit the *Star* and settled in Paris to become a literary writer.

He published two small volumes of prose and poetry in Paris in 1924 but did not receive attention in the United States until the 1925 publication of *In Our Time,* a collection of short stories. The book—which included the first appearance of Nick Adams, a recurring character who is a typically masculine, but sensitive, "Hemingway hero"—received great critical response for its understated, realistic style. The following year, he published *The Sun Also Rises,* to even greater acclaim. With its depiction of the hopelessness of postwar expatriates, the novel became a definitive rendering of the "lost generation."

Having made his name in Paris, the writer sought new places and experiences. In 1927, he divorced his wife, married Pauline Pfeiffer, and set up house in Key West, Florida. The birth of another son and the suicide of his father took him away from his work, but by 1929 he completed his well-received novel *A Farewell to Arms.* Drawn from his World War I experience, the book portrayed a disillusioned American who deserts the Italian army and tragically loses his lover. While Hemingway continued to spend time in Key West deep-sea fishing, after his last son was born in 1931 he increasingly roamed the world looking for adventure and new material. His nonfiction books *Death in the Afternoon* (1932) and *Green Hills of Africa* (1935) deal with his interests in Spanish bullfights and African big-game hunting, respectively.

Renowned as a sportsman, Hemingway also began to express social and political interests in his writing. His 1937 novel, *To Have and Have Not,* concerns a man who becomes an outlaw to feed his family during the Depression. During the Spanish Civil War (1936–39), he acted on his political beliefs by supporting the Loyalist side and reporting as a war correspondent. *The Fifth Column,* his only full-length play, takes place during the siege of Madrid; the work was published in 1938, along with the short stories from his collections *In Our Time, Men without Women* (1927), and *Winner Take Nothing* (1933). Although the play received little notice, the short stories "The Killers," "The Short Happy Life of Francis Macomber," and "The Snows of Kilimanjaro" among others are still widely appreciated. His Spanish war experience also inspired the 1940 novel *For Whom the Bell Tolls,* a less pessimistic tale emphasizing the brotherhood of mankind.

For the next several years, Hemingway was too busy to publish. After divorcing his second wife, he married Martha Gellhorn and bought an estate called La Finca Vigia outside Havana, Cuba. He spent little time there, however, choosing instead to follow the wars then raging around the world. Before the Japanese attack on Pearl Harbor, he reported from China on the Sino-Japanese War. After the United States entered World War II, he became a war correspondent for *Collier's.* In London, he met journalist Mary Welsh, who later became his fourth wife. From there he ventured to France, where he followed American troops through the Battle of the Bulge and the liberation of Paris. Hemingway became something of a legend, joining the fighting as much as reporting about it.

After the war, he returned to his life of writing and traveling. In 1950, he published *Across the River and into the Trees,* a novel about an aging army colonel that is generally considered inferior to the rest of his work. However, his next book, *The Old Man and the Sea* (1952), received the highest accolades, including a Pulitzer Prize. A chronicle of a fisherman's struggle to catch a huge marlin only to lose it to sharks, the book celebrates man's dignity and endurance as a kind of victory despite defeat. Hemingway experienced a major victory of his own in 1954, when he was awarded the Nobel Prize for literature.

Although in the prime of his life, Hemingway's enjoyment was hindered by ill health. Besides two harrowing plane crashes in Africa, he suffered spells of depression and had to be hospitalized twice at the Mayo Clinic. On July 2, 1961, Hemingway used a shotgun to commit suicide at his home in Ketchum, Idaho.

Hemingway left a lasting legacy. In 1964, *A Moveable Feast,* his memories of Paris, was published, and in 1970, the three-part *Islands in the Stream,* a novel about Bimini and Cuba, was released. His novels continue to be widely studied, and his spare, brutal style remains greatly influential. ✤

Thematic and Structural Analysis

In the opening scenes of *A Farewell to Arms* Hemingway describes the Italian landscape where Frederic Henry, an American ambulance driver and lieutenant in the Italian army, is stationed during World War I. The description is rendered with the calm, simple cadences that are Hemingway's trademark as a writer, yet it is both naturalistic and deeply symbolic. Troops passing on a nearby road raise dust—a familiar symbol of death—that covers the tree trunks and leaves. The trees lose their leaves early that year, especially with the arrival of the fall rain, another naturalistic detail that Hemingway will invest with his own meaning over the course of the book. The change of seasons leaves the country "dead with the autumn." And in a perversion of this imagery of death, Hemingway writes that the ammunition bulging beneath the fronts of the troops' capes makes them look "as though they were six months gone with child" (**book one, chapter one**).

The first chapter also depicts Frederic's early, almost uninterested relationship to the war. In **chapter two**, which jumps ahead to the following year, he and his fellow ambulance drivers move closer to the front, and Frederic lives in a villa in Gorizia, where he comes to occupy a position between the other officers and the army priest they tease at dinner. As a comrade of the officers, Frederic joins them on outings to the brothel and takes part in their bawdy conversations, yet he seems to share a bond with the quiet priest. The arrival of fall is bringing an end to heavy action, and Frederic plans an extended leave—which introduces a rhythm in the novel, its scenes alternating between warfare and "civilization." Frederic is urged by the other officers to go to "centers of culture" and "to have fine girls," while the priest invites him to visit his family in the Abruzzi, where there is "good hunting. . . . and though it is cold it is clear and dry."

Frederic returns in the spring to the same room in Gorizia and to his old roommate, Rinaldi, an army surgeon who claims to have fallen in love with a newly arrived British nurse,

Catherine Barkley (**chapter three**). Frederic must repair his friendship with the priest because his trip did not take him to the Abruzzi, as he had promised. "It was what I had wanted to do," he says to himself, but instead he had spent his vacation in "the smoke of cafés and nights when the room whirled. . . ." Although they are reconciled, Frederic's ambivalent attitude toward religion and the aspects of life represented by the priest is established. Otherwise, Frederic's surroundings remain the same as before, and he as distanced. "Evidently it did not matter whether I was there or not," he thinks in **chapter four**. Yet when Rinaldi introduces him to Catherine and her nursing colleague, Helen Ferguson, it is Frederic and Catherine who hit it off. In a painfully honest conversation, Catherine reveals that she was engaged for eight years to a man killed in France at the Somme. "They blew him all to bits," she says. As Rinaldi and Frederic return home, Rinaldi is forced to admit, "Miss Barkley prefers you to me."

In **chapter five**, Frederic moves closer to the war, but also closer to Catherine. He visits the front to analyze the duties of the ambulance drivers in the upcoming offensive. When he returns, he makes overtures to Catherine—at first rejected with a slap, then accepted with a kiss. Although Frederic adopts a gruff attitude in the narrative, when he returns home he rebuffs Rinaldi's coarse attempts at humor, thus establishing that he, at least, regards his relationship with Catherine as different from what exists between the officers and their prostitutes.

In **chapter six** Catherine asks if Frederic was truthful in saying he loved her. He readily says that he was, although noting to himself that he never said this and has no idea of loving her. He decides that she is "probably a little crazy" and thinks, "This was a game, like bridge, in which you said things." But as he goes along with the fantasy she is clearly having of her dead lover, she suddenly asks, "This is a rotten game we play, isn't it?" She places their relationship on a new level that catches Frederic off guard.

This episode is followed by a scene emphasizing the absurdity of war: While posted near the front, the ambulance drivers come across a soldier who needs treatment for a hernia but who is being denied it because his commanding officer knows that he aggravated the condition in order to escape the front (**chapter seven**). Frederic advises him to manufacture another injury that requires immediate treatment, which the man does. But before Frederic can load him in his own ambulance, the man's own regiment appears to force him to the front.

Back at the villa, Frederic prepares for dinner and although he thinks about the upcoming offensive he remains distanced: "It seemed no more dangerous to me myself than war in the movies." Still, he fantasizes about being with Catherine away from the war and in Milan. But although she expects him after dinner, he drinks too much with the other officers. When he finally tries to visit her but is told she is ill, he finds himself surprisingly "lonely and hollow."

As he leaves for the front the next afternoon, Frederic hurriedly visits Catherine, who gives him a Saint Anthony medal for protection (**chapter eight**). Although he wears it only begrudgingly, in a rare bit of foretelling he adds, "After I was wounded I never found him. Some one probably got it at one of the dressing stations." In **chapter nine** Frederic and the other members of the ambulance crew arrive at the front and, while waiting in a dugout for the action to begin, discuss the value of war. "If everybody would not attack the war would be over," says one, Manera. Frederic responds, "I believe we should get the war over. It would not finish it if one side stopped fighting. It would be worse if we stopped fighting." Another, Passini, says, "There is nothing as bad as war," but Frederic responds, "I know it is bad but we must finish it." He and another driver, Gordini, then go off in search of food before the offensive begins.

A major grants them a little pasta and cheese, but on the way back they are caught in a bombardment. They make it to the dugout safely, but when the men start to eat, their trench is hit with an Austrian bomb: Passini is killed and Frederic is injured in the head and legs. As he realizes what has happened, Frederic thinks first of aiding Passini, then of helping the three other drivers, all of whom survived, but is unable to do anything before giving himself up to treatment. A Briton arranges to take care of the abandoned ambulances as Frederic is treated. He is conscious but in shock as he is cleaned and bandaged by a glib surgeon who, once he has finished, sends Frederic off with a salute of "Vive la France"—one of the novel's first instances of confused identity. Frederic is carried away from the front in the Briton's ambulance, loaded beneath a stretcher in which a man is bleeding to death:

> The drops fell very slowly, as they fall from an icicle after the sun has gone. It was cold in the car in the night as the road climbed. At the post on the top they took the stretcher out and put another in and we went on.

At the field hospital Frederic receives visitors: Rinaldi and the priest (**chapters ten and eleven**). With Rinaldi, Frederic indulges in some barracks teasing that raises his spirits—although on the subject of the "English goddess," Catherine, the humor grows brittle—while with the priest Frederic has a more serious exchange on love and religion. "I don't love," Frederic says. "I know you will," answers the priest. "Then you will be happy." Frederic falls asleep contemplating the Abruzzi, where in the chestnut woods the "birds are all good because they [feed] on grapes and you never [take] a lunch because the peasants [are] always honored if you . . . eat with them at their houses."

Rinaldi returns later with the major, and the three get drunk in Frederic's room (**chapter twelve**). Rinaldi passes on the information that Frederic will be transferred to a new American hospital in Milan for treatment and that Catherine and Ferguson are being transferred there as well. Following a scene of drunken and affectionate leave-taking, the first book ends with Frederic making a rough passage to Milan by train.

After the chaos and absurdities of war, **book two** slowly reestablishes the pleasures of civilization. **Chapter thirteen** opens with Frederic's arrival at the new Milan hospital, but his first days there are spent in a bureaucratic tangle as the hospital is not yet ready for patients and the hospital doctor is at a clinic in Lake Como. Frederic exists on a diet of newspapers and alcohol bought by a porter he pays. When Frederic learns one morning of Catherine's arrival, he arranges for a barber to come and shave him, but the barber is surly, mistaking Frederic for an Austrian (**chapter fourteen**). Catherine arrives, and they have an impassioned greeting in which Frederic swears that he loves her and, after an interlude, says, "The wildness was gone and I felt finer than I had ever felt."

In **chapter fifteen** Frederic deals with a series of low-ranking army doctors who discuss his condition cryptically and recommend that his knee encyst over six months before being operated on. Frederic demands that the hospital doctor arrange another opinion from a higher-ranking surgeon; a major from the Ospedale Maggiore, where Frederic had previously been taken for X rays, examines him. The doctor, who has a tanned face, "laughs all the time," and takes an inordinate interest in Catherine, claims he can operate the following day and, unlike the others, accepts Frederic's invitation to have a drink. When he leaves Frederic considers himself in good hands "because he [is] a major."

Chapter sixteen begins with a slow and pensive description of Frederic and Catherine lying in his hospital bed the night before his operation. A bat flies in and out of the room, followed by a searchlight. Frederic hears soldiers from the antiaircraft battery next door, and Catherine checks to make sure the rest of the nurses, including the supervisor Miss Van Campen, are asleep. Yet otherwise they are left pleasantly to themselves. Catherine asks about Frederic's sexual past, and although she knows he lies in disclaiming it, she is appeased—the two once again agreeing to play the game "in which you said things."

Frederic comes through the surgery well and begins his recovery, visited secretly by Catherine on night duty. He is tended one day by Ferguson, who is angry that Catherine is growing so tired and warns Frederic, "You get her in trouble and I'll kill you" (**chapter seventeen**). He heeds her warning but only in asking Catherine to work fewer nights, and **chapter eighteen** opens with the line, "We had a lovely time that summer." Frederic recovers quickly, making it possible for the couple to explore the city. They experiment with wines at a local restaurant, although it "[has] no wine waiter because of the war"—a detail that throws the war into the insignificant background. Frederic describes Catherine's body and hair—which, when she shakes it free above him, gives the feeling of being "inside a tent or behind a falls"—and adds that they considered themselves married from "the first day she had come to the hospital." He offers to marry her, but she refuses, saying that regulations would then call for them to be separated. Nevertheless, they pledge themselves to each other, with Catherine claiming, "There isn't any me. I'm you," and going on to say, "You're my religion."

"The summer went that way," Frederic offers at the start of **chapter nineteen**. News from the front is good but brutal, and still distant. Frederic meets Mr. and Mrs. Meyers, an American couple who are living in Europe after Mr. Meyers, evidently a gangster, was released from prison in America. Frederic also meets a rather righteous Italian-American compatriot, Ettore, who has been decorated in the war, and with Ettore and two other compatriots who are studying to be singers, Simmons and Saunders, Frederic discusses wounds and medals—which again seems to reduce, or emblematize, the war. Ettore is "a legitimate hero who [bores] every one," Frederic later declares. For, as Catherine says, "We have heroes too. . . . But usually . . . they're much quieter." That night, as Frederic and Catherine talk softly on the hospital balcony, rain begins to fall, and in a foreshadowing exchange Catherine admits that the rain scares her: "[S]ometimes I see me dead in it. . . . and sometimes I see you dead in it." Frederic comforts her, but "outside it [keeps] on raining."

Chapter twenty shows an oppressive and tainted civilization, as Frederic, Catherine, Ferguson, and another patient named Rodgers visit the corrupt horse races with Mr. and Mrs. Meyers. Even winning horses seem to lose money, and Catherine complains that she "can't stand to see so many people," although Frederic notes that they do not see many. War then begins to reassert itself, as news from the front worsens and Frederic meets a British major who declares, "We [are] all cooked. The thing [is] not to recognize it. The last country to realize they [are] cooked [will] win the war" (**chapter twenty-one**). Yet, in a last little expression of civilization, Frederic sees a silhouette portraitist on the street and agrees to sit for a portrait—albeit with his uniform cap on. The portraitist accepts no money, saying he did the silhouette "for pleasure." The war finally summons Frederic when he reaches the hospital, where an awaiting letter informs him that he has a three-week leave in

October once he completes his physical therapy, and then he must return to the front.

That night, with some hesitation, Catherine tells Frederic that she is three months' pregnant. Imploring him not to worry, she asks if he feels "trapped," and Frederic responds that "you always feel trapped biologically." The exchange is tense until Catherine suddenly exclaims, "We really are the same one and we mustn't misunderstand on purpose." The tension dissolves, but the scene nonetheless evokes the novel's early dark image of soldiers seemingly pregnant.

"It turned cold that night," **chapter twenty-two** begins, "and the next day it was raining." Frederic comes down with jaundice, and when Miss Van Campen discovers his stash of bottles she accuses him of "producing jaundice with alcoholism" to avoid returning to the front. Frederic is allowed to rehabilitate at the hospital, but he loses his leave.

Frederic prepares to return to the war as a foggy night descends on Milan (**chapter twenty-three**). He and Catherine, spending their last hours together before Frederic must board the train, stop in an armorer's shop so that he can replace the pistol he lost when he was wounded. The shopkeeper asks if he needs a sword, but when Frederic responds that he is going to the front she admits, "Oh yes, then you won't need a sword"—thus emphasizing that the traditional accoutrements of war are now wasted. The fog turns to rain, and as Frederic and Catherine ride through the city they decide to take a room at a garish hotel. "I never felt like a whore before," Catherine says as she stares at her multi-imaged reflection in the red plush room. "[D]o we have to argue now?" thinks Frederic. But quickly she declares that she is "a good girl again," and they dine and get along better. Catherine tells Frederic not to worry about the baby. "We may have several babies before the war is over," she says, and she promises to write him "very confusing" letters to baffle the censors and preserve the privacy of their world. She then sees Frederic off in the rain (**chapter twenty-four**).

Book three opens with a reprise of the death symbolism of the novel's opening paragraph, with "wet dead leaves on the road from the rows of bare trees" near Gorizia (**chapter twenty-five**). "It's all over," says Rinaldi. He notices that Frederic acts "like a married man," and when he attempts to renew the barracks teasing about "that English girl" Frederic cuts him off. They renew their friendship, but Rinaldi is depressed, as is the priest, although he tries to insist that the war will soon end (**chapter twenty-six**). Frederic is doubtful: "[T]he Austrians will not stop when they have won a victory. It is in defeat that we become Christian."

Frederic goes the next day to the front at the Bainsizza (**chapter twenty-seven**). There he discusses military tactics with Gino, a patriotic mechanic, but he retreats from the conversation, being "embarrassed by the words sacred, glorious, and sacrifice and the expression in vain." Out on post, Frederic sees the weather turn from rain to snow and back again, and rumors abound that German troops have joined the Austrians and that an ensuing offensive will force an Italian retreat. "The word German was something to be frightened of," Frederic says. A medical officer informs him that, in the event of a retreat, as many wounded as possible will be evacuated and the ambulances will carry hospital equipment. The next night the retreat begins, but Frederic and the ambulance drivers Bonello, Aymo, and Piani are called on to load the last of the hospital equipment in the morning. They spend a final night in the villa.

In **chapter twenty-eight** they join the retreat in the rain, but the column of men and vehicles soon comes to a halt. Frederic rides with Piani, and when they are stopped he finds that, behind them, Bonello has picked up two stray sergeants and Aymo two young refugee sisters. The sergeants are surly, and the sisters, peasants who speak an unfamiliar dialect, are frightened by their surroundings and the coarse talk of the soldiers, but Frederic lets them all ride. Back in the ambulance with Piani, he dreams briefly of Catherine, "in bed now between two sheets." The retreating column moves in fits and starts, and in the morning Frederic decides it is best to leave the column and attempt to reach Udine via back roads. They come to a farmhouse and all get out, but when the sergeants attempt to loot a clock from the house, Frederic tells them to return it. The group then feasts on food and wine left behind, although the sergeants, who are nervous, would rather push on.

In **chapter twenty-nine** Aymo's ambulance becomes stuck in the mud. They have seen Austrian planes pass overhead and, just as Frederic had feared, the planes bomb the main road and the retreating column. Yet the group cannot free the mired ambulance, and when the sergeants abandon them Frederic takes out his pistol and fires at the two, wounding one while the other escapes. Bonello then executes the wounded sergeant. After another try, the four leave the ambulance and try to drive the other two across a field to another road, but those too get stuck. At this point the four strike out on foot for Udine, with Frederic giving the two sisters money and directing them toward the nearest civilians. The four attempt to brush off the incident with humor, the three Italians fondly recalling their native socialist village of Imola, but their brotherhood will not last.

The group then comes upon a line of abandoned vehicles and a bridge that has been blown up (**chapter thirty**). They walk along the river until they come to a railway bridge, and while crossing it Frederic sees a German staff car crossing another bridge down the river. Thus one small bridge has been destroyed, but a bridge on the main road has been left intact to allow the Germans to pursue the retreat. "The whole bloody thing is crazy," thinks Frederic. They follow the rail line toward Udine until they decide to cross to a side road leading to town, but as they leave the embankment they are fired on: Aymo is killed. Frederic reasons that they were probably fired on by spooked Italian soldiers, and he decides they should continue along the embankment and then attempt to enter Udine after dark.

They come to another farmhouse, and in exploring the house and barn Frederic finds himself in a reverie of his boyhood on a farm: "The hay smelled good and lying in a barn in the hay took away all the years in between." But, he adds, "You could not go back. If you did not go forward what happened?" Piani finds him and informs him that Bonello has left to surrender. Frederic and Piani feed on wine and sausages Piani found, but the wine is old and has "lost its quality and color."

After dark the two make their way back to the main retreat line toward Udine, passing a battalion of German troops undetected. Frederic is struck by the absurdity of it all: "We had walked through two armies without incident," he thinks. "The killing came suddenly and unreasonably." He and Piani join a column of retreating soldiers, but as they cross a bridge Frederic is accosted by carabinieri declaring themselves "battle police." After a brief struggle, Frederic is arrested and finds himself in a group of officers being interrogated and shot ostensibly as officers who had abandoned their troops or as Germans in Italian uniform. The questioning is ridiculous, larded with patriotic cliches, and the questioners have "that beautiful detachment and devotion to stern justice of men dealing in death without being in any danger of it." But as the carabinieri work their way toward him, Frederic picks an opportunity to run for the river; he dives in and swims away in a scene usually interpreted as an act of baptism, in which he cleanses himself of the war.

Frederic escapes by swimming underwater, and in **chapter thirty-one** he drifts down the river holding on to a large piece of timber. Although he fears drowning, he keeps his heavy wet clothes on, and when he nears the shore he makes a rough landing. Tearing the officer's stars from his sleeve and hiding them in his pocket, he begins walking south across the Venetian plain until he comes to the rail line from Venice to Trieste. Here he manages to board a train without being seen by guards, and he stows away on a rail car loaded with guns.

The symbolism of fleeing while hidden among the weapons of war is made overt in **chapter thirty-two**, which concludes book three:

> You did not love the floor of a flat-car nor guns with canvas jackets and the smell of vaselined metal or a canvas that rain leaked through, although it is very fine under a canvas and pleasant with guns; but you loved some one else whom now you knew was not even to be pretended there.

But he adds, "Anger was washed away in the river along with any obligation. . . . I was through." He thinks only of how he and Catherine will escape the country.

Book four opens literally with a new dawn (**chapter thirty-three**). Frederic drops off the train in Milan and makes his way to a wineshop, which smells of "early morning, of swept dust." The proprietor notices that the stars have been removed from Frederic's coat and offers him aid, but Frederic declines, tips him heavily, and moves off. Thus once again the presence of the war is diminishing, now emblematized by the images left by stars on fabric. Frederic talks with the hospital porter and his wife, who greet him but tell him that Catherine and Ferguson have gone to visit the resort town of Stresa. Frederic thanks them and goes to visit his American compatriot Simmons. After the tense conversation with the wineshop proprietor, this conversation begins to reestablish the relaxing tone and play of a "civilized" friendship. Simmons offers Frederic a change of clothing, and when Frederic asks about fleeing, Simmons informs him that he can row across Lake Maggiore from Stresa to Switzerland.

In **chapter thirty-four** Frederic feels like "a masquerader" in civilian clothes, but he also decides that he will forget the war because he has made "a separate peace." In Stresa he takes a room at a hotel where he has previously stayed and retreats to the bar, as the bartender is an old acquaintance. He has a few sandwiches and martinis and thinks, "I had never tasted anything so cool and clean. They made me feel civilized." He meets Catherine and Ferguson while they dine at their hotel; although Catherine is radiant, Ferguson causes a scene, calling Frederic a "dirty sneaking American Italian" for getting Catherine pregnant, and sends them away. Still, when Frederic and Catherine spend the night together, with the rain falling outside, "all other things [are] unreal." In a long passage rich with foreshadowing, Frederic reasons that "[t]he world breaks every one and afterward many are strong at the broken places. But those that will not break it kills. It kills the very good and the very gentle and the very brave impartially." In the morning the rain has stopped and they are greeted by sunlight.

That morning Frederic fishes with the barman, who offers him the use of his boat any time he wants it (**chapter thirty-five**). Later he meets with Count Greffi, a ninety-four-year-old former diplomat who represents Europe before the war. He accepts the count's invitation to play billiards, and the two have a gentlemanly conversation. Count Greffi declares that the war is "stupid" and asks Frederic what he values most. "Some one I love," Frederic answers. Greffi later tells him that love "is a religious feeling."

That night, while a storm rages outside, the barman visits Frederic and advises him that he is to be arrested in the morning (**chapter thirty-six**). Frederic and Catherine make immediate plans to flee, and the barman offers his boat. They pack, and the barman carries their bags out a back way while Frederic and Catherine slip out the front door claiming to go for a walk. The barman meets them, having also packed sandwiches, wine, and brandy. Frederic pays him for the food, but the barman insists that they send money for the boat only if they get through. He tells them how to reach Switzerland, and Frederic thanks him, but he responds, "You won't thank me if you get drowned." When Catherine asks what he has said, Frederic replies, "He says good luck." They set off.

Chapter thirty-seven describes their long overnight trip across the lake. Although Frederic rows for most of the night, they are in good spirits, and Catherine laughs when an umbrella they are using as an impromptu sail turns inside out. Before daylight it begins to drizzle, but they dodge a guard boat and reach Switzerland. Landing and talking excitedly about the breakfast they will have, Frederic says, "Isn't the rain fine? They never had rain like this in Italy. It's cheerful rain."

They are arrested after breakfast, but Frederic sticks to a story that they rowed across from Italy for "winter sport." Their abundant cash supply does much to turn the local officials in their favor, and they are sent on to Locarno, where they are granted provisional visas and where two officials even quarrel good-naturedly about whether the best winter sport is in Locarno or Montreux. Frederic and Catherine decide on Montreux, and as they proceed by carriage Catherine asks to see Frederic's "blistered raw" hands. "There's no hole in my side," he jokes, to which Catherine says, "Don't be sacrilegious."

Book five opens with a depiction of the idyllic countryside around Montreux—a depiction that echoes the novel's opening, although the scene is no longer late summer but winter (**chapter thirty-eight**). Frederic and Catherine are renting a room from a local family, the Guttingens, and Frederic thinks, "The war seemed as far away as the football games at some one else's college. But I knew from the papers that they were still fighting in the mountains because the snow would not come."

Again they discuss marriage, but Catherine says only, "I'm not going to be married in this splendid matronly state"; she does, however, promise that they will marry after the child is born. She forebodingly relates her doctor's concern about the narrowness of her hips, but they pass over the subject. Their carefree state of mind is best expressed when Frederic agrees to grow a beard. "I'll start now this minute. . . . It will give me something to do." Indeed by January Frederic has his beard and the snows are packed so hard that Catherine must wear "hob-nailed boots and a cape and [carry] a stick with a sharp steel point"—again evoking the novel's earlier dark image of the seemingly pregnant soldiers (**chapter thirty-nine**).

By March it has begun to rain, turning the snow to slush, so they decide to move to Lausanne for Catherine's impending delivery (**chapter forty**). There they have a hotel room that looks out over "the rain falling in the fountain of the garden." Yet their contented existence continues as Catherine shops for baby clothes, Frederic enjoys drinking and exercising, and together they ride frequently into the country. "We knew the baby was very close now and it gave us both a feeling as though something were hurrying us and we could not lose any time together."

Catherine's contractions begin very early in the morning (**chapter forty-one**), and after she is settled in the hospital and her labor begins in earnest she sends Frederic out to breakfast. On the way back he attempts to help a dog nosing through some garbage, but—forebodingly—there is nothing but "coffee-grounds, dust and some dead flowers." At the hospital, Frederic is permitted to dress in a gown and visit the delivery room, where he aids in administering gas to Catherine for the pain. For her labor is quite protracted and, trying to be cheerful, she wonders if she will ever have the baby. The doctor takes a break for lunch, and when he returns Frederic goes out for lunch. When he returns and dresses again for the delivery room, he finds himself appearing in the mirror "like a fake doctor with a beard." Yet the delivery is still not progressing, although Catherine, more and more drunk on gas, says, "I'm past where I'm going to die." Frederic is again sent out as the sun sets. "And this was the price you paid for sleeping together," he thinks. "This was the end of the trap."

As Frederic, alone now, begins to panic that Catherine may indeed die, the doctor comes out to recommend they do a cesarean section. Frederic agrees, and, while the doctor prepares, he revisits Catherine. He again administers gas, this time in heavier doses because it is losing its effectiveness, although doing so makes him apprehensive. "I'm not brave any more, darling," Catherine admits. "I'm all broken." "Everybody is that way," Frederic responds. "But it's awful," she says. "They just keep it up till they break you." Now she too is afraid that she will die.

Hospital staffers are drawn to the operation, but Frederic is afraid to watch and instead paces the hall, from which he can see that it is raining. When the baby is finally brought out, looking "magnificent" in the words of a doctor, Frederic thinks only that he looks like "a freshly skinned rabbit" for which he has "no feeling." He leaves the doctor still working on the baby, and when he sees Catherine again, she looks dead. Returning to consciousness, Catherine asks how the baby is, and he says, "Fine," but a nurse gives him a quizzical look. Outside he asks her about it, and she tells him that the baby was stillborn.

Frederic sits at the nurses' station and looks out the window but can see "nothing but the dark and the rain falling." "Now Catherine would die," he thinks. "That was what you did. You died. You did not know what it was about. You never had time to learn." With nothing else to be done, Frederic goes again to the café for dinner and drinks heavily, and when he returns through the rain to the hospital, he learns that Catherine has begun to hemorrhage. "I knew she was going to die and I prayed that she would not," he tells us. But, seeing her, he starts to cry. When he asks if she wants a priest, she answers, "Just you. . . . I'm not afraid. I just hate it." After she tells him that she will "come and stay with [him] nights," Frederic is sent from the room, but when she loses consciousness he returns and stays with her until she dies.

Afterward, Frederic rebuffs the doctor's invitation to drive him back to his hotel, then chases the nurses from Catherine's room and closes himself in with her body. But it is "like saying good-by to a statue." Finally he leaves the hospital and walks to the hotel in the rain. Like Catherine's body itself—once likened to that of a goddess—their love, the closest they came to faith, religion, or belief, has been destroyed. ✤

—Ted Cox

List of Characters

Frederic Henry is an American ambulance driver serving as a lieutenant in the Italian army in World War I.

Catherine Barkley is a British nurse serving in Italy in World War I, former fiancée to a British soldier killed at the Somme.

Helen Ferguson is a Scottish nurse and Catherine's friend.

Rinaldi is an Italian surgeon and Frederic's roommate, who believes he has syphilis.

The priest lives with the officers at Gorizia. He is a native of a small village in the Abruzzi.

Passini, Gordini, Manera, and Gavuzzi are ambulance drivers serving under Frederic; Passini is killed by a trench bomb, and Gordini is wounded in the attack that also wounds Frederic.

Gage and Walker are nurses at the American hospital in Milan.

Miss Van Campen is head nurse at the American hospital in Milan.

Ettore is an Italian-American wounded and decorated by Italy numerous times in World War I.

Simmons is an American singer studying in Milan.

The Meyerses are an American gangster and his wife living in Milan.

Crowell Rodgers is a British soldier wounded in the eyes and treated in Milan.

Gino is a soldier who talks about military tactics and honor with Frederic.

Piani, Bonello, and Aymo are ambulance drivers who serve under Frederic during the retreat; Aymo is killed and Bonello surrenders.

Emilio, the barman at the hotel where Frederic stays in Stresa, helps him and Catherine escape to Switzerland.

Count Greffi is an old-world European who befriends Frederic in Stresa.

The Guttingens are a family Frederic and Catherine stay with in Montreux. ✤

Critical Views

Henry Seidel Canby on Hemingway's Frankness

[Henry Seidel Canby (1878–1961) was a leading American critic of his generation. Among his many books are *Definitions: Essays in Contemporary Criticism* (1922), *Classic Americans* (1931), and *Walt Whitman* (1943). In this review of *A Farewell to Arms* from the *Saturday Review of Literature,* of which he was a long-time editor, Canby praises the frankness of the love story as presented in Hemingway's novel.]

Farewell to Arms is an erotic story, shocking to the cold, disturbing to the conventional who do not like to see mere impersonal amorousness lifted into a deep, fierce love, involving the best in both man and woman, without changing its dependence upon the senses, nor trafficking with social responsibility. It deals with life where the blood is running and the spirit active—that is enough for me. As for Hemingway's frankness of language, to object to it would be priggish. There is no decadence here, no overemphasis on the sexual as a philosophy. Rather, this book belongs with those studies of conjugal love which just now are interesting the French. If you set out to write of the love life of a man and his wife when that love life is central in their experience, why that love life is what you write about and frankness belongs to the theme.

A good Victorian, I think, would have admired the frankness of this book, and also its style, but might have felt it to be narrow to the point of triviality in its concentration. Our most skilful writers today are more interested in vivid snap shots than in cosmologies. They prefer carved peach stones to panoramas. I prefer either myself to the dull tales of "cases" so much admired a few years ago, in which fiction began to look like sociology. Hemingway does lack scope. He is attracted by the vivid; and doesn't care what is vivid so that he gets it right. It's a better way to begin than the opposite method of biographing the universe as one sees it and calling that a novel. Nevertheless, his eroticism will deserve a less specific name when he has learned how to do it. (I think he has learned) and begins to use it as a factor in synthesis. Not that *Farewell to Arms* is a "youthful," an "experimental" novel. It is absolutely done; and, even cosmically speaking, the flow of great social resolutions down and away from battle in the Alps to disillusion in the plains until all that is left of emotion is canalized into the purely personal business of love—that is a big enough theme for any novel. It is only that his stories seem to lack experience beyond the baffled, the desperate, the indifferent, the defiant so far. Which means, I suppose, that he is wise not to have written in that penetrative way of his about what has not yet engaged the imagination of his generation. In fiction, he is worthy to be their leader.

—Henry Seidel Canby, "Story of the Brave," *Saturday Review of Literature*, 12 October 1929, pp. 231–32

JOHN DOS PASSOS ON THE MERITS OF *A FAREWELL TO ARMS*

[John Dos Passos (1896–1970) was one of the most distinguished novelists of his age and the author of a celebrated trilogy of novels, *U.S.A.*, comprising *The 42nd Parallel* (1930), *1919* (1932), and *The Big Money* (1936). In this review of *A Farewell to Arms* in the radical journal *New Masses*, Dos Passos praises Hemingway's work for its artistic and historical integrity.]

Hemingway's *A Farewell to Arms* is the best written book that has seen the light in America for many a long day. By well-written I don't mean the tasty college composition course sort of thing that our critics seem to consider good writing. I mean writing that is terse and economical, in which each sentence and each phrase bears its maximum load of meaning, sense impressions, emotion. The book is a first-rate piece of craftsmanship by a man who knows his job. It gives you the sort of pleasure line by line that you get from handling a piece of well finished carpenter's work. Read the first chapter, the talk at the officers' mess in Goritzia, the scene in the dressing-station when the narrator is wounded, the paragraph describing the ride to Milan in the hospital train, the talk with the British major about how everybody's cooked in the war, the whole description of the disaster of Caporetto to the end of the chapter where the battlepolice are shooting the officers as they cross the bridge, the caesarian operation in which the girl dies. The stuff will match up as narrative prose with anything that's been written since there was any English language.

It's a darn good document too. It describes with reserve and exactness the complex of events back of the Italian front in the winter of 1916 and the summer and fall of 1917 when people had more or less settled down to the thought of war as the natural form of human existence when every individual in the armies was struggling for survival with bitter hopelessness. In the absolute degradation of the average soldier's life in the Italian army there were two hopes, that the revolution would end the war or that Meester Weelson would end the war on the terms of the Seventeen Points. In Italy the revolution lost its nerve at the moment of its victory and Meester Weelson's points paved the way for D'Annunzio's bloody farce at Fiume and the tyranny of Mussolini and the banks. If a man wanted to learn the history of that period in that sector of the European War I don't know where he'd find a better account than in the first half of *A Farewell to Arms.*

—John Dos Passos, "The Best Written Book," *New Masses* 5, No. 8 (December 1929): 16

✤

Malcolm Cowley on Battle Fiction

[Malcolm Cowley (1898–1989) was an American poet and critic and a close friend of Hemingway's. He is the author of many books, including *The Literary Situation* (1954), *A Second Flowering* (1973), and *The Flower and the Leaf* (1985). In this extract from his celebrated study, *Exile's Return* (1934), Cowley argues that the Italian retreat from Caporetto in *A Farewell to Arms* is one of the finest depictions of war in literature.]

Ernest Hemingway's hero, in *A Farewell to Arms,* is an American acting as lieutenant of an Italian ambulance section. He likes the Italians, at least until Caporetto; he is contemptuous of the Austrians, fears and admires the Germans; of political conviction he has hardly a trace. When a friend tells him, "What has been done this summer cannot have been done in vain," he makes no answer:

> I was always embarrassed by the words sacred, glorious, and sacrifice, and the expression in vain. We had heard them, sometimes standing in the rain almost out of earshot, so that only the shouted words came through, and had read them, on proclamations that were slapped up by billposters over other proclamations, now for a long time, and I had seen nothing sacred, and the things that were glorious had no glory and the sacrifices were like the stockyards at Chicago if nothing was done with the meat except to bury it. . . . Abstract words such as glory, honor, courage, or hallow were obscene beside the concrete names of villages, the numbers of roads, the names of rivers, the numbers of regiments and the dates. Gino was a patriot, so he said things that separated us sometimes, but he was also a fine boy and I understood his being a patriot. He was born one. He left with Peduzzi in the car. . . .

Two days later the Germans broke through at Caporetto.

The passage dealing with the Italian retreat from river to river, from the mountains beyond the Isonzo along rain-washed narrow roads to the plains of the Tagliamento, is one of the few great war stories in American literature: only *The Red Badge of Courage* and a few short pieces by Ambrose Bierce can be compared with it. Hemingway describes not an army but a whole people in motion: guns nuzzling the heads of patient farm horses, munition trucks with their radiator caps an inch from the tailboard of wagons loaded with chairs, tables, sewing machines, farm implements; then behind them ambulances, mountain artillery, cattle and army trucks, all pointed south; and groups of scared peasants and interminable files of gray infantrymen moving in the rain past the miles of stalled vehicles. Lieutenant Frederick Henry is part of the retreat, commanding three motor ambulances and half a dozen men, losing his vehicles in muddy lanes, losing his men, too, by death and desertion, shooting an Italian sergeant who tries to run away—but in spirit he remains a non-participant. He had been studying architecture in Rome, had become a gentleman volunteer in order to see the war, had served two years, been wounded and decorated: now he is sick of the whole thing, eager only to get away.

As he moves southward, the southbound Germans go past him, marching on parallel roads, their helmets visible above the walls. Frightened Italians open fire on him. The rain falls endlessly, and the whole experience, Europe, Italy, the war, becomes a nightmare, with himself as helpless as a man among nightmare shapes. It is only in snatches of dream that he finds anything real—love being real, and the memories of his boyhood. "The hay smelled good and lying in a barn in the hay took away all the years in between. We had lain in hay and talked and shot sparrows with an air rifle when they perched in the triangle cut high up in the wall of the barn. The barn was gone now and one year they had cut the hemlock woods and there were only stumps, dried tree-tops, branches and fire-weed where the woods had been. You could not go back"; the country of his boyhood was gone and he was attached to no other.

And that, I believe, was the final effect on us of the war; that was the honest emotion behind a pretentious phrase like "the lost generation." School and college had uprooted us in spirit; now we were physically uprooted, hundreds of us, millions, plucked from our own soil as if by a clamshell bucket and dumped, scattered among strange people. All our roots were dead now, even the Anglo-Saxon tradition of our literary ancestors, even the habits of slow thrift that characterized our social class. We were fed, lodged, clothed by strangers, commanded by strangers, infected with the poison of irresponsibility—the poison of travel, too, for we had learned that problems could be left behind us merely by moving elsewhere—and the poison of danger, excitement, that made our old life seem intolerable. Then, as suddenly as it began for us, the war ended.

When we first heard of the Armistice we felt a sense of relief too deep to express, and we all got drunk. We had come through, we were still alive, and nobody at all would be killed tomorrow. The composite fatherland for which we had fought and in which some of us still believed—France, Italy, the Allies, our English homeland, democracy, the self-determination of small nations—had triumphed. We danced in the streets, embraced old women and pretty girls, swore blood brotherhood with soldiers in little bars, drank with our elbows locked in theirs, reeled through the streets with bottles of champagne, fell asleep somewhere. On the next day, after we got over our hangovers, we didn't know what to do, so we got drunk. But slowly, as the days went by, the intoxication passed, and the tears of joy: it appeared that our composite fatherland was dissolving into quarreling statesmen and oil and steel magnates. Our own nation had passed the Prohibition Amendment as if to publish a bill of separation between itself and ourselves; it wasn't our country any longer. Nevertheless we returned to it: there was nowhere else to go. We returned to New York, appropriately—to the homeland of the uprooted, where everyone you met came from another town and tried to forget it; where nobody seemed to have parents, or a past more distant than last night's swell party, or a future beyond the swell party this evening and the disillusioned book he would write tomorrow.

—Malcolm Cowley, *Exile's Return: A Literary Odyssey of the 1920s* (New York: Viking Press, 1934), pp. 44–47

✤

Edmund Wilson on Hemingway's Characters

[Edmund Wilson (1895–1972) was perhaps the foremost American literary critic of the first half of the twentieth century. Among his many critical studies are *Axel's Castle* (1931) and *Patriotic Gore: Studies in the Literature of the American Civil War* (1962). In this extract, Wilson criticizes Hemingway's handling of the intimate emotions of the two lovers in *A Farewell to Arms.*]

The novel, *A Farewell to Arms,* which followed *Men without Women,* is in a sense not so serious an affair. Beautifully written and quite moving of course it is. Probably no other book has caught so well the strangeness of life in the army for an American in Europe during the war. The new places to which one was sent of which one had never heard, and the things that turned out to be in them; the ordinary people of foreign countries as one saw them when one was quartered among them or obliged to perform some common work with them; the pleasures of which one managed to cheat the war, intensified by the uncertainty and horror—and the uncertainty, nevertheless, almost become a constant, the horror almost taken for granted; the love affairs, always subject to being suddenly broken up and yet carried on while they lasted in a spirit of irresponsible freedom which derived from one's having forfeited control of all one's other actions—this Hemingway got into his book, written long enough after the events for them to present themselves under an aspect fully idyllic.

But *A Farewell to Arms* is a tragedy, and the lovers are shown as innocent victims with no relation to the forces that torment them. They themselves are not tormented within by that dissonance between personal satisfaction and the suffering one shares with others which it has been Hemingway's triumph to handle. *A Farewell to Arms,* as the author once said, is a *Romeo and Juliet.* And when Catherine and her lover emerge from the stream of action—the account of the Caporetto retreat is Hemingway's best sustained piece of narrative—when they escape from the alien necessities of which their romance has been merely an accident, which have been writing their story for them, then we see that they are not in themselves convincing as human personalities. And we are confronted with the paradox that Hemingway, who possesses so remarkable a mimetic gift in getting the tone of social and national types and in making his people talk appropriately, has not shown any very solid sense of character, or, indeed, any real interest in it. The people in his short stories are satisfactory because he has only to hit them off: the point of the story does not lie in personalities, but in the emotion to which a situation gives rise. This is true even in *The Sun Also Rises,* where the characters are sketched with wonderful cleverness. But in *A Farewell to Arms,* as soon as we are brought into real intimacy with the lovers, as soon as the author is obliged to see them through a searching personal experience, we find merely an idealized relationship, the abstractions of a lyric emotion.

—Edmund Wilson, "Hemingway: Gauge of Morale" (1939), *The Wound and the Bow: Seven Studies in Literature* (Boston: Houghton Mifflin, 1941), pp. 221–22

Ernest Hemingway on War

[Ernest Hemingway wrote an introduction to *A Farewell to Arms* for a reissue of the novel in 1948. Here, he comments on his lasting interest in wars and the people who fight in them.]

The title of the book is *A Farewell to Arms* and except for three years there has been war of some kind almost ever since it has been written. Some people used to say; why is the man so preoccupied and obsessed with war, and now, since 1933 perhaps it is clear why a writer should be interested in the constant, bullying, murderous, slovenly crime of war. Having been to too many of them, I am sure that I am prejudiced, and I hope that I am very prejudiced. But it is the considered belief of the writer of this book that wars are fought by the finest people that there are, or just say people, although, the closer you are to where they are fighting, the finer people you meet; but they are made, provoked and initiated by straight economic rivalries and by swine that stand to profit from them. I believe that all the people who stand to profit by a war and who help provoke it should be shot on the first day it starts by accredited representatives of the loyal citizens of their country who will fight it.

The author of this book would be very glad to take charge of this shooting, if legally delegated by those who will fight, and see that it would be performed as humanely and correctly as possible (some of the shoot-ees would undoubtedly behave more correctly than others) and see that all the bodies were given decent burial. We might even arrange to have them buried in cellophane or any one of the newer plastic materials. If, at the end of the day, there was any evidence that I had in any way provoked the new war or had not performed my delegated duties correctly, I would be willing, if not pleased, to be shot by the same firing squad and be buried either with or without cellophane or be left naked on a hill.

—Ernest Hemingway, "Introduction," *A Farewell to Arms* (New York: Scribner's, 1948), pp. x–xi

✤

JOHN ATKINS ON DISILLUSIONMENT AND SUFFERING IN HEMINGWAY'S PROSE

[John Atkins (b. 1916) is a British literary critic and author of *Aldous Huxley: A Literary Study* (1968) and *The British Spy Novel* (1984). In this extract from *The Art of Ernest Hemingway* (1952), Atkins shows how Hemingway weaves some recurring concerns—suffering, frustration, and disillusion—through *A Farewell to Arms*.]

Answering one of my questions Hemingway wrote, 'We, as citizens, are governed by fear and guided by frustration, using a non-corrected compass.' He advised me to finish it myself, apparently on the grounds that any modern citizen will know what he is getting at.

His titles alone suggest frustration. *Men without Women. Winner Take Nothing. To Have and Have Not.* Even *For Whom the Bell Tolls. The Sun Also Rises,* restored to its context in *Ecclesiastes,* breathes the same spirit. 'Vanity of vanities . . . all is vanity. . . . One generation passeth and another generation cometh; but the earth abideth forever. The sun also riseth, and the sun goeth down, and hasteth to the place where he arose.' God proposes, the temperament disposes. The Scottish poet, William Soutar, found hope in the notion that 'the earth abideth forever'. But for Hemingway God is a Gulf Stream, assimilating everything and uncaring. Hemingway is a very up-to-date

Hardy. He writes as Hardy wanted to write (philosophically, of course) after the public had learnt to stomach *Jude the Obscure.* For Hemingway men never possess women in the way they would like to—either the woman is unready or, much more likely, circumstances are unfavourable. All winners suffer at the hands of the Great Illusion. In *Farewell, Bell* and *To Have and Have Not* the lovers are frustrated by death.

All plans are nullified by death. You know that death is waiting so you know that hope is a mirage. Even those people who win their hopes are frustrated in the end for once you have got the thing you want you wish to keep it and that is impossible. The Eumenides have their eyes on you. Waiting for Catherine to die Frederic Henry realised the bitter truth, realised that until that moment his own life had been mocking him.

> Now Catherine would die. That was what you did. You died. You did not know what it was about. You never had time to learn. They threw you in and told you the rules and the first time they caught you off base they killed you. Or they killed you gratuitously like Aymo. Or gave you the syphilis like Rinaldi. But they killed you in the end. You could count on that. Stay around and they would kill you.

This is from the saddest episode in modern literature. No classical storming episode against the Fates. You could not smother your despair, your bitterness, but you had to take it lying down. Stay around and they would kill you.

No one escapes. Even when he was very happy with Catherine he seemed to have a premonition of the end. Everyone dies but the happy die first. The Lord thy God is a jealous God—thou must worship no one but Him, not even Happiness, especially not Happiness. Catherine must die because God envied her courage.

> If people bring so much courage to this world the world has to kill them to break them, so of course it kills them. The world breaks everyone and afterwards many are strong at the broken places. But those that will not break it kills. It kills the very good and the very gentle and the very brave impartially. If you are none of these you can be sure it will kill you too but there will be no special hurry.

And near the end Catherine realises this herself.

'I'm not brave any more, darling. I'm all broken. They've broken me. I know it now'.

'Everybody is that way'.

'But it's awful. They just keep it up till they break you'.

Hemingway is so explicit on the subject this chapter writes itself, or rather it has already been written. This suddenly brings me up against the embarrassing truth that a man writes his own work and what business have I to try and do it for him or explain things which he has explained better? God forgive me, I am trying to do homage to a great writer. *Farewell to Arms* is such a fine novel its mere contemplation rocks my emotion. I had better quote again. 'Catherine had a good time in the time of pregnancy. It wasn't bad. She was hardly ever sick. She was not awfully uncomfortable until toward the last. So now they got her in the end. You never get away with anything.' The message is drummed, drummed, drummed.

—John Atkins, *The Art of Ernest Hemingway: His Work and Personality* (London: Spring Books, 1952), pp. 146–48

✤

CARLOS BAKER ON THE OPENING OF *A FAREWELL TO ARMS*

[Carlos Baker (1909–1987) was the Woodrow Wilson Professor of Literature at Princeton University. He is the author of *Ernest Hemingway: A Life Story* (1969) and the editor of Hemingway's *Selected Letters* (1981). In this extract from his celebrated biographical study *Hemingway: The Writer as Artist* (1952), Baker shows how the themes in *A Farewell to Arms* are introduced in its opening passages.]

The opening chapter of Hemingway's second novel, *A Farewell to Arms,* is a generically rendered landscape with thousands of moving figures. It does much more than start the book. It helps to establish the dominant mood (which is one of doom), plants a series of important images for future symbolic cultivation, and subtly compels the reader into the position of detached observer.

"In the late summer of that year we lived in a house in a village that looked across the river and the plain to the mountains. In the bed of the river there were pebbles and boulders, dry and white in the sun, and the water was clear and swiftly moving and blue in the channels. Troops went by the house and down the road and the dust they raised powdered the leaves of the trees. The trunks of the trees too were dusty and the leaves fell early that year and we saw the troops marching along the road and the dust rising and leaves, stirred by the breeze, falling and the soldiers marching and afterward the road bare and white, except for the leaves."

The first sentence here fixes the reader in a house in the village where he can take a long view across the river and the plain to the distant mountains. Although he does not realize it yet, the plain and the mountains (not to mention the river and the trees, the dust and the leaves) have a fundamental value as symbols. The autumnal tone of the language is important in establishing the autumnal mood of the chapter. The landscape itself has the further importance of serving as a general setting for the whole first part of the novel. Under these values, and of basic structural importance, are the elemental images which compose this remarkable introductory chapter.

The second sentence, which draws attention from the mountainous background to the bed of the river in the middle distance, produces a sense of clearness, dryness, whiteness, and sunniness which is to grow very subtly under the artist's hands until it merges with one of the novel's two dominant symbols, the mountain image. The other major symbol is the plain. Throughout the substructure of the book it is opposed to the mountain-image. Down this plain the river flows. Across it, on the dusty road among the trees, pass the men-at-war, faceless and voiceless and unidentified against the background of the spreading plain.

In the third and fourth sentences of this beautifully managed paragraph the march-past of troops and vehicles begins. From the reader's elevated vantage-point, looking down on the plain, the river, and the road, the continuously parading men are reduced in size and scale—made to seem smaller, more pitiful, more pathetic, more like wraiths blown down wind, than would be true if the reader were brought close enough to overhear their conversation or see them as individualized personalities.

Between the first and fourth sentences, moreover, Hemingway accomplishes the transition from late summer to autumn—an inexorability of seasonal change which prepares the way for the study in doom on which he is embarked. Here again the natural elements take on a symbolic function. In the late summer we have the dust; in the early autumn the dust and the leaves falling; and through them both the marching troops impersonally seen. The reminder through the dust, of the words of the funeral service in the prayer-book is fortified by the second natural symbol, the falling leaves. They dry out, fall, decay, and become part of the dust. Into the dust where the troops are going—some of them soon, all of them eventually.

The short first chapter closes with winter, and the establishment of rain as a symbol of disaster. "At the start of the winter came the permanent rain and with the rain came the cholera. But it was checked and in the end only seven thousand died of it in the army." Already, now in the winter, seven thousand of the wraiths have vanished underground. The permanent rain lays the dust and rots the leaves as if they had never existed. There is no excellent beauty, even in the country around Gorizia, that has not some sadness to it. And there is hardly a natural beauty in the whole first chapter of *A Farewell to Arms* which has not some symbolic function in Hemingway's first study in doom.

—Carlos Baker, *Hemingway: The Writer as Artist* (Princeton: Princeton University Press, 1952), pp. 94–96

✤

PHILIP YOUNG ON HEMINGWAY'S SYMBOLIC USE OF RAIN

[Philip Young (1918–1991) was a professor of American literature at Pennsylvania State University. He wrote *Ernest Hemingway: A Reconsideration* (1966) and coedited *The Hemingway Manuscripts: An Inventory* (1969). In this extract, Young explores Hemingway's complex use of rain as a portent for disaster in *A Farewell to Arms.]*

A Farewell to Arms (1929), which borrows its title from a poem of that name by George Peele, reverts to the war and supplies background for *The Sun Also Rises.* For the germs of both its plots, a war plot and a love plot, it reaches back to *In Our Time.* An outline of the human arms in the novel is to be found among these early stories most people, and even the more realistic wishes of some, compliant, and bearing unmistakable indications of the troubles to come when she will appear as mistress of heroes to come, Catherine Barkley has at least some character in her own right, and is both the first true "Hemingway heroine," and the most convincing one. Completely real, once again and at once, are the minor characters—especially Rinaldi, the ebullient Italian doctor, and the priest, and Count Greffi, the ancient billiard player, and the enlisted ambulance drivers.

Chiefly, again, it is their speech which brings these people to life and keeps them living. The rest of the book, however, is less conversational in tone than before, and in other ways the writing is changed a little. The sentences are now longer, even lyrical, on occasion, and, once in a while, experimental, as Hemingway, not content to rest in the style that had made him already famous, tries for new effects, and does not always succeed. Taken as a whole, however, his prose has never been finer or more finished than in this novel. Never have those awesome, noncommittal understatements, which say more than could ever be written out, been more impressive. The book has passages which rate with the hardest, cleanest and most moving in contemporary literature.

The novel has one stylistic innovation that is important to it. This is the use of an object, rain, in a way that cannot be called symbolic so much as portentous. Hemingway had used water as a metaphoric purge of past experience before, and so Henry's emergence from the river into a new life, as from a total immersion, was not new. What is new in *A Farewell to Arms* is the consistent use of rain as a signal of disaster. Henry, in his practical realism, professes a disbelief in signs, and tells himself that Catherine's vision of herself dead in the rain is meaningless. But she dies in it and actually, glancing back at the end, one sees that a short, introductory scene at the very start of the book had presented an ominous conjunction of images—rain, pregnancy and death—which set the mood for all that was to follow, prefigured it and bound all the ends of the novel into a perfect and permanent knot.

This is really the old "pathetic fallacy" put to new use and—since there is no need to take it scientifically or philosophically, but simply as a subtle and unobtrusive device for unity—quite an acceptable one, too. Good and bad weather go along with good and bad moods and events. It is not just that, like everyone, the characters respond emotionally to conditions of atmosphere, light and so on, but that there is correspondence between these things and their fate. They win when it's sunny, and lose in the rain.

—Philip Young, *Ernest Hemingway* (New York: Rinehart & Co., 1952), pp. 60–64

JOHN KILLINGER ON HEMINGWAY'S EXISTENTIALISM

[John Killinger (b. 1933) is a professor of preaching, worship, and literature at Vanderbilt Divinity School. He is author of *The Failure of Theology in Modern Literature* (1963) and *Hemingway and the Dead Gods* (1960), from which the following extract is taken. Here, Killinger argues that the existentialism of *A Farewell to Arms* provides the explanation for Catherine (Barkley) Henry's death.]

An existential interpretation will likewise answer the question of why Catherine Henry had to die in *A Farewell to Arms.*

Catherine is one of the most likely of Hemingway's women to make a Hemingway man happy and give him a maximum amount of freedom. Throughout the novel in which she appears, she is amenable to Henry's suggestions, eager to please him. She too is simple, perhaps because she is a war nurse and has herself seen much death and brutality. In the questionable hotel in Milan—the one with the red plush furnishings which made Catherine feel like a whore for seven minutes—Henry says,

> "You're a fine simple girl."
> "I am a simple girl," she replies. "No one ever understood it except you . . . . "I'm a very simple girl."
> "I didn't think so at first," says Henry. "I thought you were a crazy girl."
> "I was a little crazy. But wasn't crazy in any complicated manner."

Yet from the beginning there is a hint of complication in their alliance. When Henry, having hardly gotten to know her, invites Rinaldi to come in to see her, Rinaldi refuses, explaining that he prefers "the simpler pleasures." The simpler pleasures are those of the whorehouse, where a man pays a fee but does not become entangled. And even after Henry's farewell to arms, which harks the reader back to Nick Adams' "separate peace," he is still not, like Nick, free from a lingering feeling of guilt:

> The war was a long way away. Maybe there wasn't any war. There was no war here. Then I realized it was over for me. But I did not have the feeling that it was really over. I had the feeling of a boy who thinks of what is happening at a certain hour at the schoolhouse from which he has played truant.

It is only when the complication is intensified by the presence of Catherine and their removal to the Swiss chalet that he ceases to feel compunctions about his truancy.

The extreme complication, however, the one demanding death for both the mother and the baby, is the baby itself. It is evident that the duties of fatherhood will threaten Henry's freedom. Catherine asks him, after telling him that she is pregnant, if he feels trapped. "Maybe a little," he answers. "But not by you."

"I didn't mean by me," she says. "You mustn't be stupid. I meant trapped at all."

Henry says, "You always feel trapped biologically."

The idea is not new here in Hemingway; in fact, it seems ingrained in his thinking. He, too, had come not too happily to fatherhood. And the hand of the author is unmistakable in "Cross-Country Snow," where Nick regrets that he must relinquish his skiing in the Alps with a male companion to return to the States for his wife to have a baby.

Catherine regrets the coming birth of the child, because she realizes the psychological constriction it puts upon Henry. More than once she apologizes for making trouble for him. He behaves more gracefully *in situation,* however, than the male in "Hills Like White Elephants," who wants his sweetheart to have an abortion so that they can go on as they have lived in the past, or than Richard Gordon in *To Have and Have Not,* who took his wife to "that dirty aborting horror," or than Mathieu in Sartre's *Age of Reason,* who planned, until Daniel offered to marry her, to have an abortion performed on Marcelle.

But the darkness of Catherine's death is a cloud spread by the author as a disguise for pulling off a *deus ex machina* to save his hero from the existential hell of a complicated life. Henry's philippic against the impersonal "they" that kills you—that killed Aymo gratuitously, that gave Rinaldi the syphilis, and that now is killing Catherine—is fine rhetoric and perhaps much in place for a universe without God in our time, but it is the author himself who is guilty of Catherine's death because of his fondness for the hero, and who makes a scapegoat of the world. The Henry who walks off into the rainy night at the end of *A Farewell to Arms* is like the Orestes who exists with the Furies in *Les Mouches*—he is alone, tormented, but very much alive in an existential sense.

Several critics have noted the recurrence of rain (or other forms of precipitation) in Hemingway's fiction, and especially in *A Farewell to Arms,* as a harbinger of disaster. Since it *is* connected with death, they generally agree that this function is diametrically opposite that of the precipitation symbol in the wasteland world of T. S. Eliot. But I believe that the rain is a symbol of fertility in Hemingway, too, though in a slightly different sense than in Eliot. To Hemingway death means rebirth for the existentialist hero in its presence, and therefore the rain, as an omen of death, at the same time predicts rebirth. The precipitation-death-rebirth combination is especially pertinent to the recurrent use of rain in *A Farewell to Arms* and of snow in *For Whom the Bell Tolls;* and a case might even be made for a theory that old Santiago, who is an existentialist in the grand style ("He was too simple to wonder when he had attained humility"), is an authentic individual because he is an old man *of the sea,* which is both a perennial reminder of man's finitude and a primordial womb symbol.

—John Killinger, "The Existential Hero," *Hemingway and the Dead Gods* (Lexington: University Press of Kentucky, 1960), pp. 46–48

JAMES F. LIGHT ON RELIGION IN *A FAREWELL TO ARMS*

[James F. Light (b. 1921), formerly dean of the College of Liberal Arts at Southern Illinois University, is the author of *Nathanael West: An Interpretative Study* (1961) and *John Williams De Forest* (1965). In this extract, Light examines the religious language and themes in *A Farewell to Arms*.]

One way of looking at Ernest Hemingway's *A Farewell to Arms* is to see its close involvement in four ideals of service. Each of these ideals is dramatized by a character of some importance, and it is between these four that Lt. Henry wavers in the course of the novel. The orthodoxly religious ideal of service is that of the Priest, who wishes to serve God but who asserts as well the broader concept of service: "When you love you wish to do things for. You wish to sacrifice for. You wish to serve." Another selfless ideal of service is that of the patriot Gino, who wishes to serve his country so fully that he is willing to die for it. A third is the code of Catherine Berkeley, who wishes to serve her lover and who sees in such service her personal substitute for conventional religion. The last is the ideal of Rinaldi, who, as a doctor, wishes to serve mankind by alleviating the wounds of war. Each is an initiate to the subordination of self, and in this they differ from the selfishness of the king and the officers who ride in cars and throw mud on the men, or from the hero

Ettore, who sees war as an accident suitable for promotion and self-glorification. In no other way, despite the contention of such a perceptive and influential critic as Robert Penn Warren, are they really initiates. They are not so in their greater discipline—Catherine is hysterical early in the novel and Rinaldi is a nervous wreck in the middle. They are not so in their talk, for though Rinaldi and Valenti, another doctor and another so-called initiate, may possess a similar "bantering, ironical tone," the Priest and Catherine are far removed from any such tone; nor do they have any greater awareness than others "of the issue of meaning in life." They act instinctively rather than intellectually, and the one instinct they have in common—the attraction toward the ideal of service—is, from the context and the conclusion of the novel, a foolish selflessness without intellectual worth.

The Priest, Gino, Catherine, and Rinaldi do, however, live by the ideal of service, and the dramatic tension of the novel is largely based on Lt. Henry's wavering toward each ideal and eventual rejection of all four. Toward the Priest's ideal, Henry's attitude is at first one of sympathy but of rejection. He does not bait the Priest with the other priest-baiters early in the novel, but neither does he stay with the Priest when the other officers leave for the whore houses near by. Nor does he visit the high, cold, dry country, the Priest's home, where he is invited to go on his leave. Instead he goes to the large cities, the ironic "centres of culture and civilization," where he lives the life of sensation and feels "that this was all and all and all and not caring." After he is wounded and has found real love with Catherine, however, Lt. Henry comes closer to the Priest, so that when he returns to duty he can reject the priest-baiting of Rinaldi and instead of going to town—and the whore houses—he can visit with the Priest. The implication apparently is that the love Henry has found in Catherine has somehow made him more sympathetic to the kind of selfless love that the Priest avows. By the end of the novel, however, Henry has thoroughly rejected the Priest and his ideal of service to God. He does, however, give that ideal a test. Where the Priest had earlier prayed for the end of the war—"I believe and I pray that something will happen. I have felt it very close"— Henry now prays that Catherine not die. Basic and repetitive in the prayer is the implication of some necessary reciprocal relation between man and God: you do this for me and I'll do this for you. Thus Henry prays: "Oh, god, please don't let her die. I'll do anything for you if you won't let her die. . . . Please, please, please don't let her die . . . . I'll do anything you say if you don't make her die." Catherine, however, does die, just as, despite the Priest's prayers, the war continues. The implication is that the Priest's ideal of service lacks reciprocity, and the knowledge of its lack is not unique to Henry. Huck Finn had earlier, in the novel that Hemingway has said is the origin of all modern American literature, felt the same flaw; for he had seen, by pragmatic test, the inefficacy of prayer, and he had discerned that the Priest's—or Miss Watson's—ideal of service was a one-way street with no advantage for the human individual. For Lt. Henry this lack of reciprocity makes for the image of a God who in his eternal selfishness is the origin of human selfishness, so that man in his selfishness most accurately reflects God. This concept of the divine selfishness is portrayed in Henry's remembrance, as Catherine is dying, of watching some ants burning on a log. Henry envisions the opportunity for him to be "a messiah and lift the log off the fire." Divinity, however, does not ease the pain of man's existence, and Henry does not save the ants. Instead, selfishly—and in so doing he is reflecting the divine selfishness which is so antithetical to the Priest's ideal of service—Henry throws "a tin cup of water on the log, so that I would have the cup empty to put whiskey in before I added water to it."

—James F. Light, "The Religion of Death in *A Farewell to Arms*," *Modern Fiction Studies* 7, No. 2 (Summer 1961): 169–70

FRED H. MARCUS ON DETAIL AND DISORDER IN *A FAREWELL TO ARMS*

[Fred H. Marcus (b. 1921) is a former professor of English at California State University. In this extract, Marcus explores the way in which Hemingway uses an

accumulation of details to create a sense of disorder and irrationality.]

A Farewell to Arms has an incredible number of details. Many appear to be trivial; others apparently bear a heavier freight of meaning. For example, the perpetual rain has been noted by almost every critic and reader of the novel. It is presumably a symbol of doom. Catherine makes allusion to her fear of rain. At the beginning of the novel rain accompanies the cholera. In the great retreat most of the withdrawal takes place in the rain. And yet the rain in Switzerland—where Catherine will die—is described by Frederic as "cheerful rain." More interesting, rain is most often thought of as a regenerative symbol, a spring rain that produces the Italian plain's rich crops and orchards. Even the winter rain bringing the cholera has its more optimistic side; the winter rain in the mountains turns to snow, a snow that ends killing and fighting and war until the following spring. Winter becomes a time of waiting in the mountains while spring unleashes the dogs of war. For Frederic and Catherine the winter in Switzerland is a waiting period; Catherine dies in the spring. Hemingway has prepared us for the inevitable. Even in the first chapter of the novel, we have met men who march toward their death, men who "marched as though they were six months gone with child." Hemingway's ironic, sometimes bitter tone can be seen in his word order and word juxtapositions. Referring to the cholera he notes that "it was checked and only seven thousand died of it in the army." At the beginning of the next chapter (Chapter II) the word "only" again serves Hemingway's purpose. The Austrians bombard Gorizia but "they did not bombard it to destroy it but only a little in a military way." Irony inheres in many of Hemingway's acute descriptions. He describes "the sudden interiors of houses that had lost a wall through shelling," a "smashed permanent bridge," steel helmets "in a town where the civilian inhabitants had not been evacuated," and Rinaldi's "holster stuffed with toilet paper."

The irrational dominated the novel. Frederic receives his wound while munching cheese; he may get a silver medal because the action was successful. During the retreat from Caporetto, he shoots at two deserters and wounds one; Bonello kills the wounded man. Shortly thereafter, Bonello deserts; so does Frederic. When the disorder of the retreat is at its worst we find Italians killing Italians while mouthing patriotic slogans. Frederic is in greater danger from Italians than from Germans; a little bridge is blown up but a bridge on the main road is untouched. The war is irrational. But what does a civilian world offer? Frederic encounters crooked racing, a purple dyed racehorse imported from France, American opera singers using Italian pseudonyms. He speaks to Meyers and Count Greffi, two old men; they survive the war almost as though it did not exist. But the young men die at an alarming rate. This world of unreason flourishes too. At the front Rinaldi, a fine surgeon, apparently has syphilis; the priest becomes disillusioned; Rinaldi says, ". . . the war is killing me" but admits his surgery has never been better.

Ironies, bitter ironies, fill the novel. Catherine describes her reason for being in Italy: "I remember having a silly idea he might come to the hospital where I was. With a sabre cut, I suppose, and a bandage around his head. Or shot through the shoulder. Something picturesque." A few moments later she adds, "He didn't have a sabre cut. They blew him all to bits." Again, the impersonal "they." Catherine later gives Frederic a Saint Anthony which she doesn't believe in. When he prepares to return to the front, he says, "Maybe I'll be back right away." Catherine responds, "Perhaps you'll be hurt just a little in the foot." Frederic adds, "Or the lobe of the ear." Catherine answers, "No I want your ears the way they are." If this is trivia, the irony is not trivial.

—Fred H. Marcus, "*A Farewell to Arms:* The Impact of Irony and the Irrational," *English Journal* 51, No. 8 (November 1962): 533–34

✤

John Stubbs on Love as a Philosophical Defense

[John Stubbs (b. 1936) is a professor of English at the University of Illinois and the author of *The Pursuit of Form: A Study of Hawthorne and the Romance* (1970).

In this extract, Stubbs examines the romantic relationship between Frederic Henry and Catherine Barkley as a defense against the senselessness of a war-torn world.]

A Farewell to Arms is Hemingway's novel about the discovery of the smallness and powerlessness of human beings in a world indifferent to their well being and about the defenses they construct to protect themselves from the crippling effects of such a discovery. Frederick J. Hoffman, in his discussion of war literature in *The Twenties,* has shown how the novel opens out from a study of war to a consideration of the hard, gratuitous quality of life in general. Other critics have discussed at length the naturalism and existentialism inherent in Hemingway's picture of man in a harsh world. What remains to be considered more fully is Hemingway's treatment of the defense Frederic Henry and Catherine Barkley put up by means of their "love" to guard themselves against the paralysis that awareness of human insignificance can produce.⟨. . .⟩

Playing roles allows them to act with kindness and strength. Nowhere is this more obvious than in Catherine's performance during her death scene. She tells Henry she is going to die, and when he takes her hand to console her, she tells him, with the anger the dying bear the living, "Don't touch me," Then recognizing the pain Henry is undergoing, she slips smoothly back into her role of lover.

> "Poor darling. You touch me all you want."
> "You'll be all right, Cat. I know you'll be all right. . . ."
> "You won't do our things with another girl, or say the same things, will you?"
> "Never."
> "I want you to have girls, though."
> "I don't want them. . . ."
> "All right," Catherine said. "I'll come and stay with you nights."

Catherine knows she is going to die. Death frightens her, and she resents it. But she sees Henry is not prepared to talk about it as openly as she is. When he tells her, "You'll be all right," he is, in effect, signalling her to keep the conversation on the level of comforting pretense. For a moment, she tries to talk realistically about their relationship as one where certain things were done and certain lines spoken according to pattern. However, his romantic responses, "Never," and, "I don't want them," indicate Henry wishes them to avoid such a candid view of their relationship and wants them instead to keep up their roles as lovers whom nothing can part. Catherine chooses to console Henry. This she does by responding to his wishes. When she tells him she will return in the night, she is deliberately taking up again her role in their game. She speaks to him the same romantic lines she required him to speak to her at the beginning of the novel. Her strength and kindness in carrying out her role playing to the end are clear. She is doing the one thing in her power to support Henry emotionally at the moment when he must take in the shattering prospect of her loss and the loss of their ordered world together.

The novel's conclusion, however, balances her kindness and courage against Henry's final realization of the inadequacy of their game to last. After Catherine has died, he returns to see her. "But after I had got them out and shut the door and turned off the light," he tells us, "it wasn't any good. It was like saying good-by to a statue." Nothing remains of their "love" after her death. Its support for him is over. The order it brought his life, like the order supplied by the army, has been destroyed. He must look directly at the indifference which the events of the outside world bear toward his private world and the ease with which they can crush it.

The balance at the end of the novel suggests the proper view for us to take toward Catherine and Henry. Ultimately their game of love and their role playing break down. The game and the roles are not strong enough to withstand the intrusion of life at its harshest. But while the game and the roles go on, they provide a means for two people to try to support each other emotionally and psychologically against the overwhelming challenge of reality that suddenly opens up before them. Through the defense of role playing, Hemingway explores both the strengths and weaknesses of his two characters. If we put aside preconceptions of what "mature love" ought to involve, we can appreciate Hemingway's psychological probing of characters looking desperately for order.

—John Stubbs, "Love and Role Playing in *A Farewell to Arms,*" *Fitzgerald/Hemingway Annual,* 1973, pp. 271, 282–83

Michael S. Reynolds on Hemingway the Intellectual

[Michael S. Reynolds (b. 1937), a professor of English at North Carolina University, is the author of *Young Hemingway* (1986) and *Hemingway: The Paris Years* (1989). In this extract from his study of *A Farewell to Arms,* Reynolds attempts to cut through many misconceptions surrounding Hemingway's work, specifically the portrayal of intellect.]

Superimposed patterns are not, ⟨. . .⟩ the only critical construction that obscures the novel. The reader must also overcome the cliché that because Hemingway opposed intellectualism he was himself unintellectual. It is an easy cliché, particularly if one ignores all evidence to the contrary. For example, Clifton P. Fadiman, an early reviewer wrote: "I have rarely read a more 'non-intellectual' book than 'A Farewell to Arms.' This non-intellectuality is not connected with Hemingway's much discussed objectivity. It is implicit in his temperament. He is that marvelous combination—a highly intelligent naïf." This representative kind of intellectual condescension reinforces the image of Hemingway the uneducated, if natural, writer who perhaps did not fully understand the dimensions of his art.⟨ . . .⟩

In the opening two chapters of the novel, which cover the first two years of the war in seven pages, Hemingway establishes the rhythmical flow of the seasons that counterpoints the violent pattern of the war. The opening two paragraphs juxtapose the natural fertility of the Italian plain with the destructive nature of the war. The plains, "rich with crops," and the "orchards of fruit trees" show the natural progress of the Italian summer, 1915. But during the summer and fall, when nature grows and ripens, the war also reaches its most destructive level of the year. The warm dry season of late summer and early fall is the time for concentrated military activity. In the winter, when deep snow buries the mountain front, both military and natural activity lie dormant, waiting to be renewed in the spring. Throughout the book there will be these two cycles in operation: the seasonal cycle of the land and the seasonal cycle of the war. The destructiveness of the war cycle is dependent upon the same seasonal weather changes that regenerate the land. This pattern is made clear in the opening chapters: the spring offensive is followed by the hard fighting of late summer and early fall; the October rains slow the fighting until the first winter snow stops it completely. Like the seasonal cycle of the plant life, the war waits for the spring to be resurrected. Frederic says in Chapter Two:

> I watched the snow falling, looking out of the window of the bawdy house, the house for officers, where I sat with a friend and two glasses drinking a bottle of Asti, and, looking out at the snow falling slowly and heavily, we knew it was all over for that year. Up the river the mountains had not been taken; none of the mountains beyond the river had been taken. That was all left for next year.

Within each cycle—fertile and destructive—Frederic finds a female relationship appropriate to the cycle in which he is involved. The destructive cycle of war has its "love" counterpart in the whorehouses that move as the front moves and that are artificially divided into enlisted and officers' houses. The inevitable product of the whorehouse relationship is venereal disease; the inevitable product of the war cycle is death. Within the fertile, natural cycle, Frederic establishes the natural love relationship with Catherine, who is the counterpart to the brothels. Frederic makes this point clear on their second meeting:

> I did not care what I was getting into. This was better than going every evening to the house for officers where the girls climbed all over you.

The relationship between Catherine and Frederic has as its natural product, Catherine's pregnancy, just as inevitably as the brothel produced Rinaldi's syphilis. And just as the destructive cycle of war produces death, so does the natural cycle of fertility produce death: the child is born dead and Catherine dies in post-operative hemorrhaging.

The parallel between Catherine's death, the destruction of the war, and the brothel's syphilis becomes overly ironic only if the reader expected a "happy ending." For the seasonal cycle of the earth is the controlling pattern and the patten ends each year with the winter death. The natural love cycle of fertility may produce life, but it also must end with death. It is in this sense that *A Farewell to Arms* is neither a war story or a love story, for love and war are but two sides of the same coin and the coin has a death-head on either side. The cycles of love and war both imitate the seasonal cycle, but love is not an alternative to war; neither love nor war is a haven from disaster. If Catherine had not died in Lausanne, she would have died later; the soldier who did not die in the mountains would have died somewhere else. As Frederic reminds the reader, sooner or later "it" or "they" will take everyone. If there is any education of the protagonist in *A Farewell to Arms,* this truism is all he learns.

—Michael S. Reynolds, *Hemingway's First War: The Making of* A Farewell to Arms (Princeton: Princeton University Press, 1976), pp. 261–65

✤

BERNARD OLDSEY ON PROSE-POETRY IN *A FAREWELL TO ARMS*

[Bernard Oldsey (b. 1923), a professor of English at West Chester State College, is the coauthor of *The Art of William Golding* (1965) and the editor of *Critical Essays on George Orwell* (1986). In this extract from *Hemingway's Hidden Craft* (1979), Oldsey comments on the effectiveness of Hemingway's use of prose-poetry in the opening of *A Farewell to Arms.]*

Whether Hemingway deliberately, consciously used the prose-poem method in composing Chapter I of *A Farewell to Arms* is impossible to say. We might remember, though, that this was Hemingway who served much of his literary apprenticeship in Paris, who utilized Proust and Villon in writing "The Snows of Kilimanjaro," and who considered using a title from Flaubert, *The Sentimental Education of Frederick Henry,* for *A Farewell to Arms.* This was the same Hemingway who wrote and spoke French and Spanish with some fluency, who contributed heavily cadenced lines of verse to American and European journals, and who moreover produced something remarkable like prose poems (resembling Max Jacob's "La Guerre" more than the rapt lines of Baudelaire) in those compressed and cadenced paragraphs and sketches that comprise *in our time.*

It remains for someone to do a thorough study of Hemingway's debt to French literary examples and methods, particularly the *poème en prose* approach. Here the concern is mainly with the manner in which he used such a method to form an introduction. Published two years before *A Farewell to Arms,* "In Another Country" employs this technique so admirably that Fitzgerald judged its opening paragraph one of the finest prose pieces he had ever read. As mentioned earlier, that paragraph (which begins "In the fall the war was always there, but we did not go to it any more," and then in a hundred words previews the entire story, imagistically and thermometrically) is the artistic precursor of the opening chapter of *A Farewell to Arms.* Both are English-language approximations of the *poème en prose* method of investing a paragraph, or a series of tightly linked paragraphs, with many of the qualities of modern poetry—such as an insistent cadence, a concatenation of images and potential symbols, and what T. S. Eliot named the objective correlative. These poetic qualities become even more discernible when the opening paragraph is arranged into one of many possible verse presentations:

> In the late summer of that year
> We lived in a house in a village
> That looked across the river and the plain
> To the mountains.
> In the bed of the river there were pebbles
> And boulders, dry and white in the sun,
> And the water was clear and swiftly moving
> And blue in the channels.
> Troops went by the house and down the road
> And the dust they raised
> Powdered the leaves of the trees.
> The trunks of the trees too were dusty
> And the leaves fell early that year
> And we saw the troops marching along the road
> And the dust rising and the leaves,
> Stirred by the breeze,
> Falling
> And the soldiers marching
> And afterwards the road bare and white
> Except for the leaves.

Chapter I of *A Farewell to Arms* consists of five such prose-poem paragraphs arranged in seasonal progression—summer dominating the first two and a half paragraphs, fall the next paragraph and a half, and winter the last paragraph (of two ironically balanced sentences). Its primary images cluster around the weather, the topography, and the historical fact of war. Thus: *sun, dust, leaves* [dropping], *rich crops, green branches* [cut], *rain, mud, permanent rain* and accompanying *cholera, river, plain, mountains, boulders, valley, vineyards; troops, artillery, motor-tractors, ammunition, rifles, cartridges.* It might be said that Hemingway here simply did what scores of World War I novelists did in setting the scene for a war story; but none of the others (not even the poet-novelist Richard Aldington in his powerfully written *Death of a Hero)* approaches Hemingway in the poetic projection of major motifs through an introductory chapter.

From their source here in the opening chapter, these motif-rays shine throughout the novel, providing unity and *claritas.* To a considerable extent, Carlos Baker has shown how this is so in his study of symbolic motifs represented by the initially mentioned mountains and plains, in terms of what happens in the highlands and lowlands throughout the novel. But we could also consider how the introductory "river" leads to the many watery scenes within the novel, in which the protagonist is wounded, in which he cleanses himself of hatred and escapes from the front, and then (by another body of water, Lago Maggiore) escapes to Switzerland, where he and Catherine live in a house where they look out over Lake Geneva. Or we could consider the motif elements of the weatherscape in this remarkable opening—where the green leaves turn dusty and then fall, where the green branches are cut, where the rain leads to cholera and death. Even Catherine Barkley's deadly pregnancy in the rain is prefigured in Chapter I as the troops, "muddy and wet in their capes," moving toward combat, carry cartridge-boxes which "bulged forward under the capes so that the men, passing on the road, marched as though they were six months gone with child."

Structurally, as well as imagistically, this poetic opening of *A Farewell to Arms* is remarkable in previewing the entire work—particularly in respect to the insistence on temporal and dramatic demarcation. The novel covers approximately two years in the narrative proper, and divides its action into five books which closely approximate the acts of classical tragedy. The first chapter, which might be called "The Masque of the Wet Death," covers about a year and is arranged in three "acts" according to the seasons. Act I, Summer, consists mainly of description and exposition, with comment on troop movement. It merges with Act II, Fall, when the leaves drop and the trees turn black: now the heavy-laden troops move to the combat zone, and the little King and his generals dash back and forth in small gray motor cars. Act III, Winter, is a truncated allegoristic conclusion charged with irony as death arrives in unexpected form: "At the start of the winter came the permanent rain and with the rain came the cholera. But it was checked and in the end only seven thousand died of it in the army." The conclusion of the novel partakes of this same ironic entrance of death in nonmilitary form, as Catherine dies in that civil bastion of security, Switzerland.

—Bernard Oldsey, *Hemingway's Hidden Craft: The Writing of* A Farewell to Arms (University Park: Pennsylvania State University Press, 1979), pp. 63–66

✣

WIRT WILLIAMS ON TRAGIC ELEMENTS IN *A FAREWELL TO ARMS*

[Wirt Williams (1921–1986) was a professor of English at California State University. In this extract from *The Tragic Art of Ernest Hemingway* (1981), Williams first compares the style and effect of *A Farewell to Arms* with *The Sun Also Rises*, then examines the nature of tragedy and helplessness in Hemingway's work.]

As an expression of the tragic, *A Farewell to Arms* differs quite visibly from *The Sun Also Rises*. It is less complicated, less a special case. And it is more concentrated. For this greater specified gravity there are many reasons: the clarity of its tragic design the greater and more poetic compactness and concreteness in its images, a generally more intense employment of many of its artistic strategies. It also differs importantly from the earlier book in that no transcendence and subsequent reconciliation are achieved. Indeed, reconciliation is counter-suggested, in both the narrative and the statement of the two decisive symbolic-metaphorical sequences of the novel—Frederic Henry walking to the hotel in the rain alone and the ants being burned to death on a campfire log. At the end there is only catastrophe, only doom: Nada—nothing—prevails unchallenged. In Hemingway's tragic equation, the stress has shifted from the possibility of individual transcendence of catastrophe by acceptance to the inescapable *fact* of universal catastrophe. If the very highest species of tragedy is that in which "inner triumph is wrested from outer defeat," *A Farewell to Arms* fails of it. This circumstance does not diminish the stunning singleness of its impact; indeed, the novel demonstrates as well as any other work that tragedy, and powerful tragedy, may be achieved without the clear triumph of spirit, without transcendence.

In the structural pattern, it is reasonable to see the duality, Frederic-Catherine, as protagonist. But it is better, perhaps, to regard Frederic as functioning alone in that role: both the larger quantity of narrative and consciousness are his, even though he and Catherine are so closely joined, and are in nearly identical situations at the beginning. The author has told us by imagistic prophecy that we are destined for tragedy before we lay eyes on them, whether or not we immediately understand the coded transmission. They are also in as typical Sartrean posture as that author's Orestes. They have appeared, come on the scene, but have not yet made the choices and taken the actions that give them the full weight of existence. Before their meeting, Frederic has divided his time between work, drink and whoring and has never made a profound choice or commitment in his life; Catherine has actually declined such a choice when presented with the opportunity of making it in an early, unrealized love affair. Both are waiting unknowingly for the choice and the action that will give definition. They play with the choice and touch but push away the defining action in the early stages of their relationship in Gorizia; it is not until after Frederic is wounded and under Catherine's care in hospital that the choice is made and the action entered. The choice is not only Sartrean; more importantly to the tragic design, it is that choice described by Bradley and Heilman as the necessary and inevitable beginning of tragedy, the turn that once taken irreversibly leads to catastrophe. The choice of Frederic and Catherine has been to love and both will be destroyed by it, though differently.

The choice made, both commit themselves totally: they move into a new dimension of sensibility and they seek to move even further. This is of course *hubris*; they are overreaching, in classic terms, trying to force more from life than it has to give, and in those same terms they are doomed. The tragedy is thus—at once and at least—Aristotelian and Heilmanic. And it also partakes of both of Frye's limiting definitions, though it expressed much more powerfully that of the omnipotent universe indifferently crushing puny humans.

That power is moving upon them unseen at the very time of their greatest happiness, their interlude in the mountains during Catherine's pregnancy. When the invisible assault culminated in catastrophe at the death of Catherine in childbirth, Henry is as destroyed as she. There appears no transcendence of reconciliation for him, only loss; his catastrophe is unredeemed and final. Thus the author's chief emphasis in this variant of his tragic equation is on the finality and inescapability of catastrophe. Life is tragic, Hemingway declares here, and nothing can alter or mitigate the fact that man is sentenced to destruction by an uncaring but functionally inimical universe.

Another view is tenable—that Frederic and Catherine have taken a triumph from their lives by their love, even though it destroys them. This implies, of course, a transcendence that precedes catastrophe, a mildly unusual but by no means unknown sequence. Yet the requisite communication of a sense of spiritual triumph is simply not in the novel. And an elaborate system of symbol, metaphor, and interior monologue insists upon the other view: that catastrophe is the ultimate end of life, and against it all attempts at amelioration are puny and futile.

—Wirt Williams, *The Tragic Art of Ernest Hemingway* (Baton Rouge: Louisiana State University Press, 1981), pp 67–69

✤

PETER BALBERT ON CATHERINE BARKLEY

[Peter Balbert (b. 1942) is a professor of English at Trinity University in San Antonio, Texas. He has written *D. H. Lawrence and the Psychology of Rhythm* (1974) and *D. H. Lawrence and the Phallic Imagination* (1989) and coedited *D. H. Lawrence: A Centenary Consideration* (1985). In this extract, Balbert disputes the views of earlier critics on the character of Catherine Barkley by claiming that she is clear in her desires and intentions.]

Which is the real Catherine Barkley? Is she the woman who mentioned that she tried but failed to prevent or abort a baby, or the woman who tries to prepare Henry for the news of her pregnancy by suggesting with pride that their instinct has triumphed and will triumph over "obstacles"? Or is she both women—a Catherine who must cope with an undesired pregnancy, but who now will teach herself (and Henry) to find positive value in the product of their passion? I believe that the more radical reading is required, with Catherine as the woman who glories in her pregnancy all the way. She seems to adjust too easily to her pregnant condition for the adjustment to be manufactured or unspontaneous. There is also a history of incompleteness in her, of opportunity squandered, which she knows would be reversed if she had a child. Catherine is no longer young, for almost a decade has elapsed since she began her involvement with her fiancé. Later she will suggest her consciousness of her age and her childlessness when she remarks to Henry that "people don't often get to my age without baby things." Immediately after her mention of contraceptive precautions she states an argument in favor of parenthood in a way which both significantly stresses the rights of her existential prerogatives, and implies, in the bareness of its announcement, that she formerly has felt deprived: "People have babies all the time. Everybody has babies. It's a natural thing." There is a logic and intensity in her mention of "natural" which must make us regard her announced contraceptive efforts with some suspicion. Catherine Barkley is an attractive woman and efficient nurse in the midst of a dirty and chaotic war; whether virginal or not before her affair with Henry, she had to be sufficiently aware of the intricacies of contraception to likely be effective at its practice; similarly, she would be familiar enough with medical personnel to have a baby aborted (at some danger to her, no doubt) if her desire for the "uncomplicated life" was really so powerful. It is more probable that Catherine knows what she wants, and that she either didn't try to stop the baby, or didn't try very hard. Surely, there must be a limit to Frederic's and Catherine's ability to pretend excitement over what they didn't want; yet only two pages after her pregnancy announcement they both excitedly picture their "son" as a lieutenant commander or general. Later they sound even less like a couple who has merely decided to make do, as Catherine remarks to Henry in a way which fuels suspicions about the baby in her: "Don't worry, darling. We may have several babies before the war is over." No, Catherine has elected to ignore the self-indulgent rules of passion and courtship in this war, just as she chooses Henry to be the man who chooses her.

—Peter Balbert, "From Hemingway to Lawrence to Mailer: Survival and Sexual Identity in *A Farewell to Arms*," *Hemingway Review* 3, No. 1 (Fall 1983): 41–42

✤

GERRY BRENNER ON FUTILITY AND IRRATIONALITY

[Gerry Brenner (b. 1937), a professor of English at the University of Montana, has written The Old Man and the Sea: *Story of a Common Man* (1991) and *Concealments on Hemingway's Works* (1983), from which the following extract is taken. Here, Brenner asserts that *A Farewell to Arms* is based upon the notions of the fundamental futility and irrationality of life.]

The sequence of Frederic Henry's major decisions reveals both his awareness of life's irrationality and the novel's underlying structure. His decision that family and country offered him no meaningful value is borne out by his disparaging references to the former and by his expatriation from the latter. His decision to stop studying architecture in Italy indicates that it obviously failed to satisfy his needs too. But that pursuit, however brief it may have been, also indicates that initially he decided to study a profession concerned with design, formal order, and tangible structures. Frederic is offhanded about his joining the Italian army and getting assigned to an ambulance unit. Yet except for medicine, no profession theoretically requires more discipline, regimentation, and obedience to orders than the military. That fact may underlie Frederic's decision to enlist, for it shows his continued search for order.

The opening chapters of the novel indicate that Frederic has served for more than a year, so he has been in the army long enough to know the gap between the military's theoretical order and reality. Futility, then, not irony, propels his remark that medicine stops the cholera epidemic only after seven thousand men die. And Catherine sees that the Italians occupy a " 'silly front'," dismantling any elevated notion of military rationality. Frederic notes early how ridiculous it was to carry a pistol that so sharply jumped upon firing that one could hit nothing. During the retreat later he sarcastically thinks that it is only as disorderly as an advance. Although Frederic falls in love with Catherine during his Milan convalescence, it is not until his next major decision, to desert the army at the Tagliamento, that he also decides to commit himself to her, seeking order and meaning now in their intimate relationship. Her death, of course, insists that nothing can immunize her against irrational forces. Neither science and Rinaldi's medical skill, nor faith and the priest's prayers, nor love and Frederic's care—none of these can keep her alive. Hemingway's borrowing the novel's title from that of George Peele's poem, then, is ironic, for he rejects the poem's conviction that "duty, faith, love are roots, and ever green"—that they offer meaningful value.

While deciding at the Tagliamento to commit himself to Catherine, Frederic makes two other decisions: to eschew thought and the processes of reasoning, and to seek order through his senses and the processes of nature. He tells himself that he was made not to think but to eat, to drink, and to sleep with Catherine.

Frederic's justification for the former decision rests upon more than the travesty of rationality he hears the battle police at the bridge declaim. After all, the military landscape abounds in irrationality. Pleasure palaces on the front lines? An offensive campaign in the mountains? Gas masks that fail to work? An ambulance unit of anarchists? Bridges not blown to slow the German offensive? Medals of honor for victims of accidents? No less irrational is the social landscape Frederic portrays. Were it not for the pain in his legs, his arrival at the Milan hospital would be Chaplinesque: an unkempt nurse, unprepared rooms, unmade beds, unanswered bellcords, and an absent doctor. Puzzled and angry he asks how there can be a hospital with no doctor. Just as the fixed horse races violate one activity over which chance and unpredictability should rule, so too do Frederic and Catherine violate the idea of a hospital: their romance transforms a ward for physical suffering into a haven of sensual gratification. The "comic opera" of their interrogation by the Swiss police at Locarno further justifies Frederic's derision of reason, aped as reason is by absurd civil formalities. His refrain throughout the last third of the novel, that he does not want to think, does not reflect a wish to escape or delay responsibility. It expresses his belief that thinking is a poor remedy for human problems.

Frederic's decision to embrace sensory experience and nature's processes is just as poor a remedy. Nature is no more orderly, controllable, or predictable than reason. Frederic's shrapnel-filled legs fail to raise his temperature. But Miss Gage patronizingly tells him that foreign bodies in his legs would inflame and give him a fever. Contrary to Miss Van Campen's belief, he cannot keep from contracting jaundice. Neither can Catherine prevent conception, assuring Frederic that she did everything she could, but that nothing she took made any difference. More to the point, Catherine's narrow hips thwart nature's reproductive cycle. And the umbilical cord, rather than nourishing fetal life, becomes a hangman's noose. At the novel's end neither spring nor rain will bring their normal regeneration.

The British major at the club in Milan tells Frederic how to respond to their world: "He said we were all cooked but we were all right as long as we did not know it. We were all cooked. The thing was not to recognize it." Stripped as Frederic has been of virtually everything that would give him reason to continue living, when Catherine dies he cannot avoid seeing that he too is "cooked." And that prompts his next-to-last decision, to tell his story.

—Gerry Brenner, *Concealments in Hemingway's Works* (Columbus: Ohio State University Press, 1983), pp. 28–30

✣

ROBERT W. LEWIS ON REAL AND FALSE LANGUAGE

[Robert W. Lewis (b. 1930), a professor of English at the University of North Dakota, is the editor of *Hemingway in Italy and Other Essays* (1990) and the author of *Hemingway on Love* (1965) and A Farewell to Arms: *The War of the Words* (1992), from which the following extract is taken. Here, Lewis studies the effect of real and false uses of language in *A Farewell to Arms* as a means of portraying character.]

The theme of real and false uses of language is elsewhere present in those episodes concerning Frederic and Catherine's private life. In writing about Frederic's character, I have already noted the many instances in which he lies to or misleads others. Lying, of course, is deliberate "misuse" of language if the standard of judgment is honesty and truth. But Frederic is a pragmatist, not an idealist. His standard of judgment is success in achieving some practical or desired end, whether control of his ambulance unit or seduction of Catherine.

Early on we are alerted to the importance to the narrator of the precise use of language, as in the vivid description in chapter 1. Further, we learn that he is bilingual in Italian and English. Later we learn that his use of French was good enough to make one Italian officer think he was French, and frequently in the course of the story he notes little confusions of speech, as when Rinaldi is struggling with English and takes literally what Helen Ferguson means only rhetorically. Frederic is quite aware of the power of language, and in one scene with the Italian-American officer we learn that Ettore's power derives directly from his fluency in two languages. He speaks idiomatic English (for instance, "So long. Don't take any bad nickels"), and he disparages the American opera singer Ralph Simmons because "He can't pronounce Italian." Similarly, Ettore's fluent Italian gives him an edge on Frederic in getting promoted. Frederic doesn't "know the Italian language well enough . . . to be a captain."

Language is power when Frederic does know Italian well enough to mistranslate for ignorant Catherine the barman's warning about drowning to "Good luck," and in his first meetings with Catherine, they are aware of the *way* in which they communicate. In their very first conversation, they have a hostile exchange that Catherine redirects by asking him, "*Do* we have to go on and talk this way?" At their next meeting, he picks up on an idea suggested earlier by Catherine's head nurse. *We* and *they* are identified by our languages, and the British head nurse asks Frederic why he didn't join up with *us*, his fellow English-speakers, and not the Italians, who, despite their "beautiful language" are not "us" and not welcome as visitors at her hospital. When that evening Catherine rebuffs Frederic's advances, he regroups by using the idea of the head nurse, who chauvinistically derogated the Italians and accepted Frederic simply on the basis of their common language. As noted before, his "line" invites Catherine's pity merely because his work precludes speaking English—his mother tongue. The appeal is "nonsense" to Catherine, but it works and she yields to his kiss.

At several points Frederic thinks similarly of the Italians, with their theatrical helmets and ways of saluting, and the regulation requiring him to wear a ridiculously designed pistol gives him "a vague sort of shame when I met English-speaking people"—that is, the British and other Americans, who presumably are united in their ethnicity and language and contrast to the theatrical Italians. Frederic reinforces this motif here by noting that the English gas mask he carried was "a real mask"—a wonderful oxymoron beyond its literal meaning. For a character who often dissembles, this little joke is revealing.

After Catherine extracts a lying admission of love from Frederic, she then drops the game and gently admonishes him:

"Please let's not lie *when we don't have to*" (my emphasis). And she reveals her own careful ear for language when she tells him that he pronounces "Catherine" differently from the way her dead fiancé did. Frederic is after all not, as revealed by language, the surrogate of her beloved. And when do they "have to" lie? They do not begin lying *together* until after his wounding, when he finds himself truly in love with Catherine and they begin "making" love. On the eve of his operation, Catherine counsels him, if not to lie, at least to conceal the truth of their love when, under anesthesia, he may "get very blabby." But Frederic says that he won't talk, and Catherine admonishes him for bragging, which is a kind of lying.

Their talk then shifts to a humorous inquiry by Catherine of Frederic's prior lovemaking experience. When he denies having any, Catherine says:

> "You're lying to me."
> "Yes."
> "It's all right. Keep right on lying to me. That's what I want you to do."

And that is what he does in this comic scene, except when Catherine signals that she really wants to know the truth in answer to one question: Does a prostitute and her client say they love each other? Frederic tells the truth: yes, if they want to. But then, unknown to Catherine, he lies and says that *he* never told another woman he loved her. Catherine is deceived, and the lie elicits her profession of love for him. But what is the moral impact of the lie? Is it one of those which Catherine had earlier acknowledged as a "white," or forgivable, even necessary, lie? And how is one to understand the narrator's (Frederic's, of course) curious interruption of their dialogue with a sentence of description of the sunrise *outside* his room and a sentence that echoes Catherine's earlier observation that her bathing him and giving him an enema in preparation for his operation had made him "clean inside and outside"? Cleanliness of mind is also at issue, and Frederic's successful lie belies Catherine's love that she then avows, now convinced that Frederic is sincere. In their first lovemaking she had repeatedly asked for confirmation of his love. Now his white lie convinces her. She has cleaned his body inside and outside, and she is finally very happy.

—Robert W. Lewis, A Farewell to Arms: *The War of the Words* (New York: Twayne, 1992), pp. 131–33

✤

PETER MESSENT ON LOST IDENTITIES IN *A FAREWELL TO ARMS*

[Peter Messent is the author of *New Readings of the American Novel* (1990) and *Ernest Hemingway* (1992), from which the following extract is taken. Here, Messent explores the confusing world of identity in *A Farewell to Arms.*]

The issue of identity is foregrounded from the start in *A Farewell to Arms* in the questions raised about the name and status of its central protagonist. The first chapter has 'we' as its subject. The narrator is part of a larger and undefined group, presumably (and in retrospect) those members of the division who 'lived in a house in a village'. In the second chapter a shift takes place as a reference to 'our house' is replaced by a narrow focus on the individual subject: 'I was very glad.' In the next two chapters the definition of the subject continues to waver between 'I' and 'we', but it is noticeable that an intensified use of the former pronoun (nine times in the first paragraph) at the start of chapter 3 marks the protagonist's return from a winter's absence. This can be linked to his realisation, soon to be formulated, that professionally speaking he has not been missed: 'It evidently made no difference whether I was there . . . or not.' The stress on his presence as a subject can be seen as a defensive ploy in a situation where his suspicions of his own irrelevance to a larger process and activity are about to be confirmed. It is only at this point that we learn the protagonist's army function. It is also here, in chapter 4, that we learn that he is not an Italian (though his American nationality is not given until the next chapter). There is, then, a very gradual early release of information about this subject and the sense of his dislocation and potential futility is strong, both in the detail given about his professional role and in that general sense of the random and coincidental exemplified when he gives his reason for joining the Italian army.

The text initially withholds the name of this central protagonist. Both the mechanics and Catherine call him by his professional rank ('Signor Tenente', 'Tenente'). Even this can confuse the English-speaking reader who may not know the Italian for lieutenant and may be thrown onto the wrong track by the 'Signor' which initially precedes it. He is eventually defined as Mr Henry by Miss Ferguson at the start of chapter 5, and Catherine repeats this in a peculiarly formal manner (given that he now calls her 'darling') in the next chapter. His first name, or rather the Italian variant of it, Frederico, is not given until the end of chapter 7. It is here, though, that the potential confusion between first and last names that already exists is compounded as Bassi, who first identifies the protagonist by his full name during a drunken conversation in the mess, plays with its two elements: 'He said was my name Frederico Enrico or Enrico Federico?' Only at the start of Book Two, when he has already experienced that sense of non-being that occurs with his wounding—'I felt myself rush bodily out of myself'—does the protagonist name himself unequivocally as Frederic Henry; the reader having been further confused meanwhile by the major's repetition of Bassi's 'Federico'. As Scott Donaldson notes, 'People are always misspelling Frederic Henry's name, and no wonder: only once in the book does Hemingway supply it, in full, and those who know him best usually do not call him by any name at all.'

This sense of uncertainty concerning the identity of the major protagonist is continued in different forms as the book proceeds. His youth, inexperience and lack of awareness are implicit in the 'suggestive' term of affection, 'baby', which Rinaldi constantly employs in conversation with him, and in the way that Catherine, the priest and others refer to him as a silly (or poor or good) 'boy'. This linked to a stress on an unformed and provisional quality to his selfhood which constantly recurs. For the notion of role-playing and false identity is one consistently associated with Frederic. Even before we have been given that first clear naming of him in the hospital, reference has been made to him, to achieve speedy medical treatment, as 'the only son of the American Ambassador' and then, jokingly, as 'the American Garibaldi'. This type of deliberate misidentification goes together with less jocular forms of the same activity. Catherine gets him to play the role of her dead fiancé when, 'nearly crazy', she first meets him and has him ventriloquising the words she would have that financé speak. The barber in the hospital mistakes him for an Austrian. During the retreat the battle police mistake him for a German agitator in an Italian uniform. Frederic, in fact, 'is continually being mistaken for someone he is not'.

—Peter Messent, *Ernest Hemingway* (New York: St. Martin's Press, 1992), pp. 56–58

NANCY R. COMLEY AND ROBERT SCHOLES ON CATHERINE BARKLEY'S SELF-SACRIFICING NATURE

[Nancy R. Comley is a professor of English at Queens College of the City University of New York and the coeditor of *Writing and Reading Differently* (1985). Robert Scholes, a professor of English at Brown University, is a leading literary critic and theorist. Among his books are *Structuralism in Literature: An Introduction* (1974), *Fabulation and Metafiction* (1979), and *Textual Power* (1985). In this extract from *Hemingway's Genders* (1994), Comley and Scholes explore the passive nature of Catherine Barkley in her relations with Frederic Henry.]

Catherine Barkley seems to be aware of the predominantly physical basis of Frederic Henry's "love," for, on the morning of her operation, as she performs her professional task of making him "clean inside and out," she questions him about the behavior of whores, coming to understand the rules of that game as one in which the whore "says just what he wants her to." Her questions are not idle, for she is exploring a new role for herself as a sexual partner. Thus she vows to "do what you want and then I'll be a great success." When he asks her to come to bed with him again and she agrees, he will no longer be her dead soldier-lover, but she will be his live nurse-whore. She offers herself, saying, "There isn't any me any more. Just what you want."

Such apparent compliance and self-erasure have seemed appalling to many readers (though some male critics have found Catherine an ideal woman), but it is possible to read this episode in a slightly different way. We might, for instance, see Catherine not as erasing herself so much as assuming a role in a game of sex and love that allows her to transfer her affections to a man other than her dead fiancé. She assumes the role of whore as a means of escaping profoundly restrictive cultural codes—those of her social code, which require of her a chastity suitable to a chosen profession, which forbid sexual relations between military nurses and their charges. As a "bad girl," she can learn to enjoy illicit sex in stolen moments. Switching back to her role as nurse, she becomes the ministering angel, the mother-Madonna, the body slave, thus enacting a primal male fantasy of modern culture that Frederic Henry, supine on his bed of pain and pleasure, amply equipped with wine and brandy, is in the ideal position to enjoy.

As Klaus Theweleit points out, "one of the pervasive male fantasies in our society concerns sexual relations with nurses. . . . It is that staple food on which, for example, Hemingway's [*A Farewell to Arms*] feeds. Equally well known is the fact that nurses refuse to conform to the images of them projected in male fantasies. . . . When all is said and done, the patient doesn't desire the nurse as a person, but as an incarnation of the caring mother, the nonerotic sister. Indeed, that may be why nurses are called 'sister' in so many countries."

Where soldiers are concerned, the hospital situation is "highly conducive to that fantasized (non)love situation" because a person's wound "usually impedes his lovemaking ability." And, with his individual right taken away, the soldier is in effect "reduced to the status of a child" and thus focuses his "needs for mother-child and sibling relations onto the sister-nurses" (Theweleit). As a Red Cross nurse, Agnes von Kurowsky was "forbidden to carry on serious romances, even to be alone with a gentleman caller." Henry Villard, who was hospitalized in the room next to Hemingway's when he was in the same condition as Frederic Henry, concurs with Agnes' statement that a hospital affair such as that described in the novel "was totally implausible."

But what a delicious fantasy, what a safe kind of regression to a time before one must confront the realities of an adult world. In *A Farewell to Arms,* Frederic Henry's childish status is reiterated throughout. His roommate Rinaldi's favorite epithet for him is Baby, and the priest and Catherine, among others, call him a good boy or urge him to be one. There are echoes here of Agnes von Kurowsky's pet names for Ernest, as found in her letters to him: Kid, Bambino, my boy, or Maestro Antico—"the inversion of the same concept" (Villard). But this is the fantasy of a sexualized Oedipal child who desires the mother-sister-nurse. In the "real world" of the novel the characters enact the fantasy of the author. This fantasy does not end with Frederic Henry's recuperation and his return to the more adult world of the war, for his desire is always to return to the waiting Catherine, the faithful and loving mother-mistress. He is the hungry child who would devour his mother, and Catherine willingly abdicates from what little self she has to give herself over to his desires. Together they try to establish a world of their own, a world of oneness, as they move further from society into a life centered in the womblike protection of a Swiss featherbed.

—Nancy R. Comley and Robert Scholes, *Hemingway's Genders: Rereading the Hemingway Text* (New Haven: Yale University Press, 1994), pp. 37–39

✣

Works by Ernest Hemingway

Three Stories & Ten Poems. 1923.

in our time. 1924

In Our Time: Stories. 1925.

The Torrents of Spring: A Romantic Novel in Honor of the Passing of a Great Race. 1926.

Today Is Friday. 1926.

The Sun Also Rises. 1926.

Men without Women. 1927.

A Farewell to Arms. 1929.

Death in the Afternoon. 1932.

God Rest You Merry Gentlemen. 1933.

Winner Take Nothing. 1933.

Green Hills of Africa. 1935.

To Have and Have Not. 1937.

The Spanish Earth. 1938.

The Fifth Column and the First Forty-nine Stories. 1938.

For Whom the Bell Tolls. 1940.

Men at War: The Best War Stories of All Time (editor). 1942.

Voyage to Victory: An Eye-witness Report of the Battle for a Normandy Beachhead. 1944.

The Portable Hemingway. Ed. Malcolm Cowley. 1944.

Selected Short Stories. c. 1945.

The Essential Hemingway. 1947.

Across the River and into the Trees. 1950.

The Old Man and the Sea. 1952.

The Hemingway Reader. Ed. Charles Poore. 1953.

Two Christmas Tales. 1959.

Collected Poems. 1960.

The Snows of Kilimanjaro and Other Stories. 1961.

The Wild Years. Ed. Gene Z. Hanrahan. 1962.

A Moveable Feast. 1964.

By-Line: Ernest Hemingway: Selected Articles and Dispatches of Four Decades. Ed. William White. 1967.

The Fifth Column and Four Stories of the Spanish Civil War. 1969.

Ernest Hemingway, Cub Reporter. Ed. Matthew J. Bruccoli. 1970.

Islands in the Stream. 1970.

Ernest Hemingway's Apprenticeship: Oak Park 1916–1917. Ed. Matthew J. Bruccoli. 1971.

The Nick Adams Stories. 1972.

88 Poems. Ed. Nicholas Gerogiannis. 1979, 1992 (as *Complete Poems*).

Selected Letters 1917–1961. Ed. Carlos Baker. 1981.

The Dangerous Summer. 1985.

Dateline, Toronto: Hemingway's Complete Toronto Star *Dispatches, 1920–1924.* Ed. William White. 1985.

The Garden of Eden. 1986.

Complete Short Stories. 1987.

Remembering Spain: Hemingway's Civil War Eulogy and the Veterans of the Abraham Lincoln Brigade. Ed. Cary Nelson. 1994.

Works about Ernest Hemingway and *A Farewell to Arms*

Baker, Sheridan. *Ernest Hemingway: An Introduction and Interpretation.* New York: Holt, Rinehart, 1967.

Benson, Jackson J. *Hemingway: The Writer's Art of Self-Defense.* Minneapolis: University of Minnesota Press, 1969.

Beversluis, John. "Dispelling the Romantic Myth: A Study of *A Farewell to Arms.*" *Hemingway Review* 9 (1989): 18–25.

Cooper, Stephen. *The Politics of Ernest Hemingway.* Ann Arbor, MI: UMI Research Press, 1987.

Dekker, George, and Joseph Harris. "Supernaturalism and the Vernacular Style in *A Farewell to Arms.*" *PMLA* 94 (1979): 311–18.

Denis, Brian. *The True Gen: An Intimate Portrait of Ernest Hemingway by Those Who Knew Him.* New York: Grove Press, 1988.

Donaldson, Scott. *By Force of Will: The Life and Art of Ernest Hemingway.* New York: Viking, 1977.

———. "Censorship and *A Farewell to Arms.*" *Studies in American Fiction* 19 (1991): 85–93.

———, ed. *New Essays on* A Farewell to Arms. Cambridge: Cambridge University Press, 1990.

Elliott, Ira. "*A Farewell to Arms* and Hemingway's Crisis of Masculine Values." *Literature Interpretation Theory* 4 (1993): 291–304.

Engelberg, Edward. "Hemingway's 'True Penelope': Flaubert's *L'Education Sentimentale* and *A Farewell to Arms.*" *Comparative Literature Studies* 16 (1979): 180–216.

Fleming, Robert E. *The Face in the Mirror: Hemingway's Writers.* Tuscaloosa: University of Alabama Press, 1994.

Ganzel, Dewey. "*A Farewell to Arms:* The Danger of Imagination." *Sewanee Review* 79 (1971): 576–97.

Gladstein, Mimi Reisel. *The Indestructible Woman in Faulkner, Hemingway, and Steinbeck.* Ann Arbor, MI: UMI Research Press, 1986.

Glasser, William A. "*A Farewell to Arms.*" *Sewanee Review* 74 (1966): 453–67.

Grebstein, Sheldon. *Hemingway's Craft.* Carbondale: Southern Illinois University Press, 1973.

Griffin, Peter. *Along with Youth: Hemingway, the Early Years.* Oxford: Oxford University Press, 1985.

Grimes, Larry E. *The Religious Design of Hemingway's Early Fiction.* Ann Arbor, MI: UMI Research Press, 1985.

Gurko, Leo. *Ernest Hemingway and the Pursuit of Heroism.* New York: Crowell, 1968.

Hatten, Charles. "The Crisis of Masculinity, Reified Desire, and Catherine Barkley in *A Farewell to Arms.*" *Journal of the History of Sexuality* 4 (1993): 76–98.

Hays, Peter L. *Ernest Hemingway.* New York: Continuum, 1990.

Hovey, Richard B. "*A Farewell to Arms:* Hemingway's *Liebstod.*" *University Review* 33 (1966–67): 93–100, 163–68.

———. *Hemingway: The Inward Terrain.* Seattle: University of Washington Press, 1968.

Kert, Bernice. *The Hemingway Women.* New York: Norton, 1983.

Lee, A. Robert, ed. *Ernest Hemingway: New Critical Essays.* Totowa, NJ: Barnes & Noble, 1983.

Lewis, Robert W., ed. *Hemingway in Italy and Other Essays.* New York: Praeger, 1990.

Lockridge, Ernest. "Faithful in Her Fashion: Catherine Barkley, the Invisible Hemingway Heroine." *Journal of Narrative Technique* 18 (1988): 170–78.

Lynn, Kenneth S. *Hemingway.* New York: Simon & Schuster, 1987.

McCarthy, Paul. "Chapter Beginnings in *A Farewell to Arms.*" *Ball State University Forum* 10, No. 2 (1969): 21–30.

McIlvaine, Robert M. "A Literary Source for the Caesarean Section in *A Farewell to Arms.*" *American Literature* 43 (1971): 444–47.

McNeely, Trevor. "War Zone Revisited: Hemingway's Aesthetics and *A Farewell to Arms.*" *South Dakota Review* 22, No. 4 (1984): 14–38.

Mellow, James R. *Hemingway: A Life without Consequences.* Boston: Houghton Mifflin, 1992.

Nagel, James, ed. *Ernest Hemingway: The Writer in Context.* Madison: University of Wisconsin Press, 1984.

Noble, Donald R., ed. *Hemingway: A Revaluation.* Troy, NY: Whitston, 1983.

Prescott, Mary. "*A Farewell to Arms:* Memory and the Perpetual Now." *College Literature* 17 (1990): 41–52.

Reynolds, Michael S. *Hemingway: The American Homecoming.* Oxford: Basil Blackwell, 1992.

———. *The Young Hemingway.* Oxford: Basil Blackwell, 1986.

Rosen, Kenneth, ed. *Hemingway Repossessed.* Westport, CT: Praeger, 1994.

Rovit, Earl. *Ernest Hemingway.* New York: Twayne, 1963.

Scafella, Frank, ed. *Hemingway: Essays of Reassessment.* New York: Oxford University Press, 1991.

Solotaroff, Robert. "Sexual Identity in *A Farewell to Arms.*" *Hemingway Review* 9 (1989): 2–17.

Spilka, Mark. *Hemingway's Quarrel with Androgyny.* Lincoln: University of Nebraska Press, 1990.

Stephens, Robert O. "Hemingway and Stendhal: The Matrix of *A Farewell to Arms.*" *PMLA* 88 (1973): 271–79.

Wagner, Linda W., ed. *Ernest Hemingway: Six Decades of Criticism.* East Lansing: Michigan State University Press, 1987.

Waldhorn, Arthur. *A Reader's Guide to Ernest Hemingway.* New York: Farrar, Straus & Giroux, 1972.

Watson, William Braasch. "Investigating Hemingway." *North Dakota Review* 60 (1992): 1–27.

Weber, Ronald. *Hemingway's Art of Non-fiction.* New York: St. Martin's Press, 1990.

Wexler, Joyce. "E.R.A. for Hemingway: A Feminist Defense of *A Farewell to Arms.*" *Georgia Review* 35 (1981): 111–23.

Whitlow, Roger. *Cassandra's Daughters: The Women in Hemingway.* Westport, CT: Greenwood Press, 1984.

Whittier, Gayle. "Childbirth, War and Creativity in *A Farewell to Arms.*" *Literature Interpretation Theory* 3 (1992): 253–70.

Williams, David. "The Poetics of Impersonality in *A Farewell to Arms.*" *University of Toronto Quarterly* 59 (1989–90): 310–33.

Wylder, Delbert E. *Hemingway's Heroes.* Albuquerque: University of New Mexico Press, 1969.

Index of Themes and Ideas